A. C. Cruikshank

The young cook's guide

A text-book on cookery

A. C. Cruikshank

The young cook's guide
A text-book on cookery

ISBN/EAN: 9783744786065

Printed in Europe, USA, Canada, Australia, Japan

Cover: Foto ©Lupo / pixelio.de

More available books at **www.hansebooks.com**

THE YOUNG COOK'S GUIDE

A TEXT-BOOK ON COOKERY.

PREPARED FOR

THE YOUNG WOMEN'S CHRISTIAN ASSOCIATION

OF BROOKLYN,

BY

MISS A. C. CRUIKSHANK.

BROOKLYN, N. Y.
PRESS OF COLLINS & DAY, 138 LIVINGSTON STREET.
1893.

To my Mother,

My first teacher in culinary art,

this book is affectionately

dedicated.

THE question of what we shall eat is one that deserves our earnest study and thought. The bountiful Giver of all good has, in this our native land, placed at our hand the greatest variety of wholesome foods from which to choose. He who makes the wisest choice will reap a reward in health, and ability to enjoy.

DR. ALLEN.

CONTENTS.

INTRODUCTION.   PAGE
Course A., ... 13
 "   B., ... 15
 "   C., ... 17
Mottoes for Course A., ... 19
 "   "   "   B., ... 21
 "   "   "   C., ... 23
How to use this book, ... 25
Abbreviations, ... 26
Table of measures and weights, . . . 26
Time table for cooking, ... 27
Fire, ... 29
Making and care of a fire, ... 30
Food, ... 32
Digestion, ... 36
Cooking, ... 42
Boiling, ... 42
Simmering, ... 44
Steaming, ... 44
Roasting, ... 45
Broiling, ... 46
Braising, ... 48
Frying, ... 48
Sautéing, ... 50
Larding, ... 51
Stirring, Beating, Folding, ... 51
Bread crumbing, ... 52
Boning, ... 53
Care of food, ... 56
Setting the table, ... 58

CONTENTS.

	PAGE
Waiting on table,	59
Clearing the table,	60
Washing dishes,	60
Recipes,	64
Soups,	64
Fish,	76
Meat,	90
Poultry and game,	106
Meat and fish sauces,	113
Sweetbreads,	118
Vegetables,	120
Grains,	133
Griddle cakes and waffles,	136
Bread,	138
Rolls,	143
Biscuits, gems and muffins,	146
Eggs,	153
Salads,	160
Sandwiches,	166
Croquettes,	168
Fritters,	173
Puddings and desserts,	175
Jellies,	190
Pudding sauces,	192
Cake,	195
Pastry and pies,	205
Ice creams and sherbets,	210
Fruit,	218
Beverages,	223
Sundries,	226
Odds and ends,	236
Invalid cooking,	247

INTRODUCTION.

OUR best literature abounds in culinary allusions; as Shakepeare's "Epicurean cooks sharpen with cloyless sauce his appetite," so Burns' poem on that great Scotch dish—a haggis, "Great Chieftan of a Pudding Race," serve as examples.

Among the poets, Shelley was indifferent to his food, and read while he ate. Byron starved himself for fear of obesity, while many another author has starved from necessity. But that most of our literary friends shine best at table is proved, were proof needed, by the charming accounts of Roger's Breakfasts and Lady Blessington's Dinners. The famous "Kit Kat Club" gave its name to some scarcely less famous mutton pies.

While it is possible "to cultivate Literature on a little oat-meal," for there are proteids in the suggestion, what lover of good things does not envy the old London authors those delightful repasts at the quaint taverns Leigh Hunt writes of in "The Town."

Boswell and Mrs. Thrale so carefully noted Dr. Johnson's eating, while seated admiringly in his company, one wonders if they had time for their own meals.

Perhaps like a certain old lady of our acquaintance they dined surreptitiously, appearing with delicate lack of appetite at table and creating much sympathy until betrayed by a gormandizing shadow on the pantry door, just before dinner time.

Often the only history of a people is preserved in the cooking utensils of their domestic life.

How eagerly collectors seek for Indian pottery or search the buried cities for traces of an earlier civilization, while every household utensil which preserves for us the customs of our ancestors is of value as illustrating the history of Colonial times.

A modern knowledge of the chemistry of food would prohibit the use of some of these quaint utensils but one may well lament the going out of the Dutch oven and basting spit of earlier days.

Carlyle's immortal dyspepsia may follow Emerson's immortal pie, but Sidney Smith's salad " 'Twould tempt the dying anchorite to eat."

Kept in countenance by such worthy examples, it is well for us to prepare for a banquet together. Gathered about a daintily spread board and served with dishes to be evolved out of the recipes and instructions to follow in these pages, one may with propriety " confess to a partiality for paté and a tenderness for truffles."

"B."

IN preparing this volume it has not been with any desire to add to the number of valuable books on the subject, but merely to have in convenient form, the material needed in the class work, of the Cooking Department, of the Young Women's Christian Association of Brooklyn. Should it prove helpful to any outside of our work it will more than fulfill its mission.

THE AUTHOR.

COURSE OF INSTRUCTION

AT THE

Young Women's Christian Association,

BROOKLYN.

FIRST COURSE—COURSE A.

PRINCIPLES OF COOKING.

Lesson I.—A Quick Breakfast.

Making and care of the fire. Measuring. Coffee. Oatmeal. Toast. Scrambled Eggs.

Lesson II.—Boiling.

Boiled Mutton. Gravy. Boiled Potatoes. Mashed Potatoes. Apple Sauce. Bread Pudding.

Lesson III.—Simmering.

Soup Stock. Vegetable Soup. Croutons. Bread Crumbs. Minced Meat on Toast. Cottage Pie. Stewed Prunes.

Lesson IV.—Steaming.

Beef Stew. Dumplings. Steamed Rice. Apple Snow Balls. Lemon Sauce.

Lesson V.—Roasting.

Roast Beef. Gravy. Franconia Potatoes. White Sauce. Creamed Cabbage. Scalloped Apple.

Lesson VI.—Broiling.

Beef Steak. Pan Broiled Chops. Potato Soup. Cottage Pudding. Lemon Sauce.

Lesson VII.—Frying.

Fried Potatoes. Split Pea Soup. Griddle Cakes. Doughnuts.

Lesson VIII.—Bread.

Bread.

Lesson IX.—Invalid Tray.

Soft Boiled Egg. Dropped Egg. Beef Tea. Gruel. Milk Toast. Egg Nog. Tea. Bird's Nest. Baked Apples. Lemon Jelly.

Lesson X.—Stirring. Beating. Folding.

Omelet. Soft Molasses Cookies. Chocolate Layer Cake. Boiled Icing.

SECOND COURSE--COURSE B.

PRINCIPLES ELABORATED.

Lesson I.

Baked Fish. Hollandaise Sauce. Fruit Meringue.

Lesson II.

Chicken Fricassee. Cranberries. Creamed Potatoes. Molasses Fruit Cake.

Lesson III.

Fancy Rolls. Creamed Salt Fish. Apples for Luncheon.

Lesson IV.

Oyster Soup. Creamed Oysters. Baked Crackers. Crackers and Cheese. Little Pigs in Blanquets. Floating Island.

Lesson V.

Ham Omelet. Lyonnaise Potatoes. Ginger Suet Pudding. Fruit Suet Pudding. Foamy Sauce.

Lesson VI.

Roast Chicken. Giblet Gravy. Potato Salad. French Dressing. Lunch Cake.

Lesson VII.

Fried Codfish. Tartar Sauce. Sponge Cake. Philadelphia Ice Cream.

Lesson VIII.—A Luncheon.

Mock Bisque Soup. Fish Gratin. Meat Balls. Escaloped Sweet Potatoes. Lettuce Salad. Frozen Apricots. Chocolate.

Lesson IX.

Fried Oysters. Broiled Oysters. Apple Pie. Pastry.

Lesson X.

Chicken Salad. Mayonnaise. Sandwiches. Snow Pudding. Soft Custard.

THIRD COURSE—COURSE C.

FANCY COOKING.

Lesson I.

Bisque of Lobster. Codfish Croquettes. Orange Charlotte.

Lesson II.

Pureé of Salmon. Blanquette of Salmon. Potato Border. Coffee Ice Cream.

Lesson III.

Turbans of Flounder. Romoulade Sauce. Spinach à la Crême. Waffles. Lemon Syrup.

Lesson IV.

Dresden Patty Cases. Creamed Ham. Apple Fritters. Foamy Sauce.

Lesson V.

Veal Cutlet à la Provencale. Spaghetti. Tomato Sauce. Orange Layer Cake. Ornamental Frosting.

Lesson VI.

Fancy Omelets. Lady Cake. Bavarian Cream.

Lesson VII.

Potato Croquettes. Stuffed Eggs. Café Parfait. Chantilly Baskets.

Lesson VIII.—A Dinner.

Consommé. Lobster Cutlets. Chicken Croquettes. Hamburgh Steak. Maître d'Hotel Butter. Creamed Potato Balls. Scalloped Turnips. Egg Salad. Orange Sherbet. Café Noir.

Lesson IX.

Mutton Rechauffé. Fruit Baskets. Lemon Meringue Tarts.

Lesson X.

Larded Sweetbreads. Omelet Soufflé. Ice Cream.

These courses may be changed as the needs of the classes require.

MOTTOES.

COURSE A.

Lesson I.

Let all things be done decently and in order.
—*Bible.*

Lesson II.

Do unto others as you would that they should do unto you.—*Golden Rule.*

Lesson III.

A soup fast boiled is a soup half spoiled.—*Ruskin.*

Lesson IV.

A little thing, a sunny smile,
  A loving word at morn,
And all day long the sun shone bright,
The cares of life were made more light,
  And brighter hopes were born.—*C. L. Hill.*

Lesson V.

Whatever thy hand findeth to do, do it with thy might.

Lesson VI.

He doth much that doth a thing well.
—*Thomas à Kempis.*

Lesson VII.

A recipe for to-day :
"Take a dash of water cold
And a little leaven of prayer,
And a little bit of sunshine gold
Dissolved in the morning air;
Add to your meal some merriment,
And a thought for kith and kin,
And then as your prime ingredient,
A plenty of work thrown in."

Lesson VIII.

A little leaven leaveneth the whole lump.—*Bible.*

Lesson IX.

A merry heart doeth good like a medicine.—*Bible.*

Lesson X.

"Success is doing your best every day."

COURSE B.

Lesson I.

There is always a best way of doing every thing, if it be to boil an egg.—*Emerson.*

Lesson II.

What men want is not talent, it is purpose; in other words, not the power to achieve, but the will to work.—*Bulwer-Lytton.*

Lesson III.

"Little by little all tasks are done,
So are the crowns of the faithful won,
So is heaven in our heart begun."

Lesson IV.

Over and over again
  The brook through the meadow flows,
And over and over again
  The ponderous mill-wheel goes.
Once doing will not suffice,
  Though doing be not in vain,
And a blessing failing us once or twice
  May come if we try again.

Lesson V.

So here hath been dawning another blue day;
Think, wilt thou let it slip useless away?
Out of eternity this new day is born;
Into eternity at night will return.—*Carlyle.*

Lesson VI.

" Plant blessings, blessings will bloom ;
Plant hate and hate will grow ;
You can sow to-day, to-morrow will bring
The blossom that proves what sort of thing
Is the seed, the seed that you sow."

Lesson VII.

Only live your life and your duty do,
And be brave and strong and steadfast and true.
—*Luella Clark.*

Lesson VIII.

" For the common deeds of the common day,
Are ringing bells in the far away."

Lesson IX.

Art little? Do thy little well, and for thy comfort know,
Great men can do their greatest work, no better than just so.—*Goethe.*

Lesson X.

" Not enjoyment, and not sorrow,
Is our destined end or way ;
But to act that each to-morrow
Find us farther than to-day.
Build to-day then strong and sure,
With a firm and ample base,
And ascending and secure
Shall to-morrow find its place."

COURSE C.

Lesson I.
Each day is a fresh beginning,
Every morn is the world made new.
—Susan Coolidge.

Lesson II.
Go make thy garden as fair as thou canst,
   Thou workest never alone ;
Perchance he whose plot is next to thine
   Will see it, and mind his own.
—Robert Collyer.

Lesson III.
Let us be content, in work,
To do the thing we can, and not presume
To fret because it's little.—*E. B. Browning.*

Lesson IV.
" Be more cheerful, do not worry,
   There is time enough to do
Every day the daily duties
   That your father sendeth you,
And to find some little moments
   For heart music fresh and new."

Lesson V.
"What are you doing from day to day
   As the precious moments slip away?
Oh, use them for some good endeavor,
For moments gone are gone forever.
Like pearls that slip from a broken clasp,
   Life's moments slip from our careless grasp."

Lesson VI.

Like the star,
That shines afar,
Without haste
And without rest,
Let each man wheel with steady sway,
Round the task that rules the day,
And do his best.—*Goethe.*

Lesson VII.

True worth is in being, not seeming,
In doing each day that goes by,
Some little good—not in dreaming,
Of great things to do by-and-by.
—*Alice Cary.*

Lesson VIII.

Be faithful and active and earnest;
In idleness never sit down:
The better the dark cross you carry,
The brighter will sparkle your crown.
—*Wm. Johnson.*

Lesson IX.

"Rest is not quitting the busy career,
Rest is in fitting of self to one's sphere.
'Tis living and serving the highest and best,
'Tis onward unswerving—and this is true rest."

Lesson X.

Each triumph of the right,
Each action grand and pure,
Written in lines of light,
Forever shall endure.—*Amasa Lear.*

HOW TO USE THIS BOOK.

" Trifles make perfection ; but perfection is no trifle."

Turn to the recipe you wish to use.

See that you have everything in the house needed for it.

Turn to the front of the book and read the few remarks on how to cook it; if baked, look for remarks on baking; if boiled, on boiling; if rolled in crumbs, egg and crumbs, remarks on breading, etc.

Look up the time-table for cooking it.

See that the fire is in proper condition.

Lay all the utensils and ingredients on one table in the coolest part of the kitchen.

Follow the recipes explicitly.

Measure with great care and accuracy.

The last thing before cooking, read the recipe through slowly and think if you have put in everything mentioned.

Should the result be a failure, it is from some mistake on your part, as every recipe in the book has been tested many times in the author's classes, by pupils knowing as little about cooking as you do. Remember, practice makes perfect.

ABBREVIATIONS.

tbsp.	stands for	tablespoonful.	m.	stands for	minute.
tsp.	"	teaspoonful.	h.	"	"	hour.
ssp.	"	"	saltspoonful.	qt.	"	"	quart.
c.	"	"	cupful.	pt.	"	"	pint.
hp.	"	"	heaped.	lb.	"	"	pound.
spk.	"	"	speck.	oz.	"	"	ounce.

TABLE OF MEASURES AND WEIGHTS.

4 ssp. . . . = 1 tsp.	4 c. flour . . . . . = 1 lb.
3 tsp. . . . = 1 tbsp.	2 c. solid butter . = 1 lb.
4 tbsp. . . = ¼ c.	2 c. gran. sugar . = 1 lb.
4 gills . . = 1 c.	3 c. meal . . . . . = 1 lb.
2 c. . . . . = 1 pt.	1 hp. tbsp. butter = 2 oz.
2 pt. . . . = 1 qt.	1 hp. tbsp. sugar = 1 oz.
4 qt. . . . = 1 gallon.	2 c. solid meat . = 1 lb.
8 qt. . . . = 1 peck.	1 tbsp. liquid . . = ½ oz.

A speck is what you can put on a quarter-inch square surface.

Measure salt, pepper, soda and spices level spoonfuls. Measure everything else, including cream of tartar, rounded.

TIME-TABLE FOR COOKING.

BAKING.

Bread	45 m.
Biscuits and rolls	10 to 15 "
Loaf Cake	30 " 40 "
Fruit Cake	3 " 4 "
Pies	30 " 40 "
Potatoes	30 " 40 "
Sweet Potatoes	30 " 40 "
Beef rare	8 to 10 m. per lb.
Mutton, well done	15 " " "
Chickens	$1\frac{1}{4}$ to 2 h.
Turkeys, 10 lb.	$2\frac{1}{2}$ " 3 h.
Grouse	30 m.
Quail	15 " 20 "
Fish, 4 to 6 lbs.	45 " 60 "

BOILING.

Potatoes	20 " 30 m.
Sweet Potatoes	15 " 20 "
Rice, sweetbreads, spinach	15 " 20 "
Winter vegetables, except beets and grains	1 to 2 h.
Fish	6 to 10 m. per lb.

BROILING.

Chickens	20 m.
Shad	20 "
Steak and chops	6 to 10 m.
Chops in paper	10 m.

FIRE.

"All the heat which we generate for household purposes is caused by the chemical action of air upon fuel."

Air consists mainly of two gases, oxygen and nitrogen, with a minute quantity of carbonic acid gas and watery vapor. Oxygen constitutes one-fifth of the air and nitrogen four-fifths. Coal, wood, charcoal, kerosene oil and gas are composed of a solid substance called carbon, or a gas called hydrogen. Fuels that contain both are called hydro-carbons.

Oxygen has a powerful attraction for these two substances, and at a certain temperature, called the "burning point," combines with them and produces combustion and heat; the result of this combustion is carbonic acid gas and watery vapor. Thus we scratch the match, the heat of the friction ignites the sulphur, and with the burning match we light the paper, and that in turn warms and lights the wood. As the fire burns a chemical change takes place in the fuel, and we have as a result gas, smoke and ashes; the energy which has been stored up in the fuel has been liberated in what we call heat and fire. The gases, carbonic acid and smoke, formed from burning fuel are poisonous and must have some escape from the room. We must also have a good supply of air, as one pound of wood requires nearly six pounds of air to burn it, and one pound of mineral coal over nine pounds of air.

MAKING AND CARE OF A FIRE.

"Well begun is half done."

Open all the dampers, close the lids and slides, turn over the grate; let it stand a minute for the ashes to settle. Open the lids, brush the ashes from the inside of the stove; clean out the oven, remove the ashes and set the grate safely and surely. Put in loose rolls of paper half way up the grate, cover with shavings or chips, then a layer of larger pieces of wood. Put on the covers, brush the entire stove and blacken it, but do not polish it yet; open all the draughts, light a piece of paper and push under the grate so as to light the back part; light the front also. Now polish the top of the stove and all around, put on the water for cooking, watch the course of the flame that you may choose the hottest part: when the paper is burned, open one lid at a time, push the wood down evenly, add another good layer of wood and a thin layer of coal. Be careful to leave no holes for the coal to fall, through the wood, onto the grate. As the coal burns up add more coal, being careful not to let any lie on the top of the inside of the stove, and *never have it about the fire box or near the lids.* It is wasteful and you will not have as hot an oven as with a low, clear fire. When the blue flame has left you may close the dampers, as this shows that the gas has passed off. The fire is at its best when first kindled; when bright red most of its heat has passed away.

To keep a fire for baking for several hours, add a little coal at a time and keep the under part free from ashes by raking a little, occasionally keeping some of the draughts open.

Do not rake a whitey-red fire, you will put it out.

Put on a very few coals, open all the draughts, let it kindle well, add a very little more coal, and when that has kindled rake carefully and add more coal.

To keep a fire for hours without using add a little fresh coal, and after a few moments close the dampers.

If any thing be spilled on the stove rub well with paper at once.

Use a paper bag from the grocers on your hand when polishing the stove and burn up when done.

Sift all ashes well, remove all slate and clinker and sprinkle well with cold water.

FOOD.

Food is anything that supports or nourishes life.
Every movement, breath, thought, results in waste.
This waste must be supplied.

A certain amount of heat, also, is needed to support life; if the temperature of our bodies vary a few degrees the result is fatal.

Our food should supply material for growth, repair, and warmth.

Food has been classified viz:

> Nitrogeneous or Albuminous, also called Protieds.
> Carbonaceous.
> Water—which cannot be ranked strictly with either group.

Nitrogeneous Foods contain nitrogen, and supply material for growth and repair.

Carbonaceous Foods contain carbon, and supply material for heat.

Water assists in dissolving and carrying the food through the body, regulates the temperature by throwing off the heat through the skin in perspiration, and through the lungs, and constitutes three-fourths of the entire weight of the body.

The blood, bones, nails, muscles, are largely composed of water.

There are also minerals found in small quantities in most of our food, which serve to build up certain tissues.

Chloride of sodium, or common salt, iron, potash, sulphur, magnesia, lime, phosphorus, silica.

Lime is found in the bones and teeth.

Phosphorus is found in the brain.

Silica is found in the hair and nails.

Iron gives color to the blood.

NITROGENEOUS OR ALBUMINOUS FOODS—PROTIEDS.

The typical food of this class is albumen, white of egg; so called from a Latin word, meaning "the white."

Protied is from a Greek word, meaning "first," because nitrogen is always found in the living cells which are the beginning of life.

Albuminous foods consist of eggs, lean meat, fish, milk, wheat, peas, beans, corn, oatmeal. The albumen in meat is in the juice; in egg, the white; also a little in the yolk; in flour, the gray, sticky substance called gluten; in milk the curd; in peas and beans it is called vegetable caseine.

Egg albumen coagulates and becomes a solid white substance when placed in water at a temperature of 166°.

Blood albumen coagulates at a temperature of 160°.

Cold water merely holds it in solution.

CARBONACEOUS FOODS.

These foods are classed under three heads, viz:

Starch,
Sugar,
Fats.

The starches and sugars are classed together and called Carbo-hydrates. As they are the chief heat producing foods they need abundance of oxygen to burn them, as the fire needs plenty of air to burn the fuel.

Starch—is found in large quantities in grains, seeds, vegetables, and is also found in the fruits, leaves and stems.

Sago,
Tapioca, } 83 per cent. starch.
Arrowroot,

Rice and fine wheaten flour, 76 per cent. starch.
Rye, 71 " " "
Scotch oatmeal, 63 " " "
Peas, 51 " " "
Potatoes, 15 " " "

In the seeds it is the stored up energy of the summer.

Starch consists of minute grains of different size and shape; potato grains being largest, wheat smaller, parsnips and turnips still smaller. Starch is a snow-white powder and is stored up in cells with very thin walls of an albuminous juice, which is not affected by cold water. Hot water heats the juice and causes the starch grains to burst.

Sugar differs from starch in that it can be easily dissolved in cold water and has a sweet taste. It is found in both plants and animals. Our supply comes entirely from plants, their saps, juices, fruits and seeds. The two principal varieties are cane sugar and grape sugar. Nearly all of our common sugar is obtained from the sugar cane.

Grape sugar composes the main bulk of honey and is found in large quantities in raisins, plums, figs, and other fruits.

Sugar, under the action of ferment, is decomposed; grape sugar is the quickest to change, as cane sugar, by the agency of acids, must first be changed to grape sugar before it will ferment.

Milk sugar, found in milk, is similar to cane sugar, and is changed, when taken as food, into grape sugar.

FATS AND OILS.

These are the principal heat-giving foods, being about eighty per cent. carbon and ten per cent. hydrogen; when they come in contact with oxygen are burned with great intensity and yield much heat.

One pound of suet requires three pounds of oxygen for perfect combustion, while one pound of starch requires but one and two-tenth pounds of oxygen.

They are also the chief material of adipose tissue, and a certain amount is needed to give beauty to the form.

Our fats and oils are obtained from animals and vegetables.

Suet, mutton tallow, and lard, are from beef, mutton and pork; cod liver oil, from the liver of the cod; butter and cheese from milk; olive oil, from the fruit of the olive; and many nuts and seeds have it in large quantities.

The fats are stored up in the system against a time of need, and supply warmth and activity during abstinence from food.

DIGESTION.

Digestion is the process by which food is changed into a liquid and becomes a portion of the blood; the source from which the entire system draws for all its needs. There are three distinct processes which take place:

    First—in the mouth.
    Second—in the stomach.
    Third—in the intestines.

As the food passes through the body it meets with five digestive juices which act on the different foods.

1. Saliva—acts upon starchy food.
2. Gastric—acts upon nitrogenous food.
3. Bile—acts upon fat and retards decomposition.
4. Pancreatic—acts upon fat.
5. Intestinal—has the power of all the other juices.

1. *Saliva.*—When the food enters the mouth it meets the first digestive juice, which is the saliva, and is stored in three pairs of salivary glands, which lie under the ear, side of the throat and under the chin. The saliva is alkaline, is mostly composed of water, to dilute the food; a small quantity of saline matter to season the food and give it the taste; and a peculiar substance, called ptyalin, which forms less than one five-hundredth part of the whole saliva. It is this substance that changes the starch into sugar, and after a while the sugar into lactic acid. This saliva also froths easily and so carries oxygen with the food into the stomach.

It is of the greatest importance that the food should be thoroughly masticated and moistened with the saliva, that the first step in digestion be thorough. Salt and seasoning cause the saliva to flow; the thought or sight of some attractive dish will cause the mouth to water. Care should be taken not to waste or throw away what nature has provided and needs for constant use.

Saliva has no effect on nitrogenous foods.

2. *Gastric juice.*— The food, after leaving the mouth, passes into the stomach, which is a sort of pouch, the walls of which consist of three muscular coats, which move in different directions, and produce a churning motion; from the inside wall, pours a fluid called gastric juice. It is always acid, hydrochloric, and contains a minute quantity of a fermenting substance, called pepsin, which is a powerful digestive agent, and is obtained for medicinal purposes from the stomachs of hungry little pigs.

As the food is rolled round and over in the stomach, the surface of it is exposed to this juice, which acts upon the nitrogenous food, and changes the gluten and fibrin of flesh to a semi-fluid state, and melts the fat, but does not change it. The stomach, through the minute veins spread over the entire inner surface, absorb some of the perfectly digested food, while the rest passes in this fluid state into the smaller intestines.

3. *Bile.*

4. *Pancreatic.*—A few inches from the entrance of the food into the small intestine, two small tubes open, one from the liver, bringing bile, the other from the pancreas, pouring in pancreatic juice.

These juices are alkaline, and attack the undigested starch, and reduce the fats and oils to minute particles.

5. *Intestinal.*—From the walls of the intestines flow the intestinal juice, which is also alkaline. Although the bile, pancreatic, and intestinal juices are all alkaline, they act upon the sugar, changing it to lactic acid, and the contents of the intestines quickly become acidulous, thus completing the digestion of portions of nitrogenous food not fully digested in the stomach. As the food passes through the intestine a portion of it is absorbed through the veins which line the intestines, and part is taken up by fine tubes arising in the intestinal coats, called lacteals, which finally gather into a tube, called the thoractic duct, and by this duct conveyed into large veins above the heart; it then passes through the heart into the pulmonary artery, thence into the lungs. The worn out tissue is also carried to the lungs and there burned up, or thrown out of the system with the undigested food. As the blood enters the lungs it is purple, but the oxygen it meets there changes it to red vitalized blood, and burns up the impurities which are thrown out of the lungs at every breath, in carbonic acid gas and watery vapor; the same products as are formed by the combustion produced in a fire. The oxygenized blood passes through the heart again and enters the great artery, from which it is carried by smaller arteries all through the system. From this supply each little cell and tissue draws such material as it needs for repair; for the cells and tissues are constantly wearing out and need building up.

As we must keep the grate free from ashes if we want a bright fire, so we must keep the body free from useless matter if we wish to be healthy.

The bowels, kidneys, lungs, skin, are constantly throwing off the waste of the system, and need to be in good working order, or disease follows. The lungs should be well filled with pure air, the pores of the skin kept open by frequent bathing, the kidneys and bowels perform their work regularly. We may stop the supply of food for days without injury, but let the waste material fail to be removed for one day, it will poison the system and disease will follow.

All of our food is not digested, some of it passing through the intestines unchanged, and is carried with the innutritious portion from the body through the bowels.

NUTRITIOUS AND INNUTRITIOUS FOODS.

Nutritious foods are those which can be digested, and so made part of the blood, from which the system is repaired and built up. Innutritious foods are those which cannot be digested, either from their nature, or by improper combinations, or have been made indigestible by cooking.

Albumen is the great supply of the nervous system, but if through improper cooking it is hardened and toughened, as in the case of a so-called hard boiled egg, it passes through the body, giving little, if any, nutriment.

While the system needs a large amount of nutritious food, it needs also a certain quantity of innutritious food to furnish bulk for the digestive organs to work upon. But to load the system with food that will take hours to digest, if digested at all, is to weaken and wear out the digestive organs, and bring on a train of troubles that may take years to remove.

Plain, wholesome food, well cooked and attractively served, will help to create a healthy appetite and good digestion.

Regular periods for eating are also necessary, that in the intervals there may be time for the building up of the parts that have been wasted during the digestive process.

DAILY REQUIREMENT OF FOOD.

No definite rule can be laid down for the regulation of individual diet, as climate, age, occupation and temperament must all be considered. "What is one man's meat is another man's poison," so that while certain proportions of different foods have been recommended, every intelligent person must learn from experience what is best for them; but our diet must combine different kinds of food material in order to repair all the parts. It is necessary to remember the different properties of food to proportion them, so as each may supply what is lacking in the other. That it must be attractive, both in appearance and odor, is of importance; and to produce this result we try to bring out tempting flavors, for food that tastes good, gives more nourishment, so that seasoning is a great help to·digestion.

Eggs and milk are both types of perfect food, containing all the necessary elements; but many persons can not eat eggs, and milk is not agreeable to all. Certain elements are needed by all in every

DAILY REQUIREMENT OF FOOD. 41

day's portion, and the best rules are those that include animal as well as vegetable diet. The proportion for growing persons is one part nitrogenous and four parts carbonaceous. For grown persons one part nitrogenous to five or six parts carbonaceous. A fair average ration per day is, perhaps:

Bread........................1 lb. 10 oz.
Fat........................1 to 2 oz.
Rice (cooked)..................$\frac{1}{2}$ lb.
Flesh........................$\frac{1}{2}$ lb.

Bread and potatoes contain no fat and require butter to make them palatable; we serve milk or cream with oatmeal, cheese with crackers or maccaroni; thus we supply to each what is lacking. Laboring people, and those working in the open air a good deal, need wholesome food in large quantities; those who spend much of their time in close, heated rooms, need more easily digested food, containing a great amount of nutriment. Avoid fat and much animal food in the summer, using grains, green vegetables and fruits; they are far better than any drugs to purify the system. Those who find it difficult to make both ends meet, should choose the foods containing the most nutriment for the least money. Indian meal, flour, rye flour, wheat, oatmeal, barley, beans, are among the best.

COOKING.

To cook is to prepare or dress; to boil, bake, or roast.

We cook our food to make it more palatable and digestible, and thus make it more nutritious.

Some of our food has already been prepared by the heat of the sun, such as lettuce, radishes, fruits, etc.; some can be cooked in their own juices, such as tomatoes, spinach; and still others have been hardened during the ripening process, such as grains, and need to be cooked in a liquid, that they may be swollen and softened.

The tender fibres of steak, fish, poultry, etc., are improved by cooking with intense dry heat, such as we have in roasting or broiling, which keep all the juices and nutriment in the meat.

A free circulation of air while cooking, also improves and develops certain flavors, as in the case of broiled, roasted or toasted food.

BOILING.

Boiling is the process of cooking our food in a boiling liquid.

Water is the liquid most generally used.

We first boil or cook the water before cooking the food in it.

Water is composed of two gases; eight parts oxygen, one part hydrogen. As the water boils the gases escape and give it a flat taste; therefore, to improve the flavor of food *it should always be freshly boiled.* When water is put in a pan on the fire as it becomes heated, small bubbles rise and burst just before they reach the surface, causing a very slight motion. This is called simmering, and the temperature is $180°$. In a little while the bubbles rise, breaking and bubbling above the surface. The water is now boiling and the temperature is $212°$. If we increase the heat and cause the water to boil furiously, we will find that the temperature is the same, so that if water boils it is a waste of fuel to make it boil any harder, as the food will not be cooked any quicker. Milk boils at $196°$ as it is much thicker than water.

If we will remember the following effect of hot and cold water on the elements of food, we will be able to reason for ourselves which to use, without constantly running to find out from some other quarter.

Cold water draws out the juices, albumen and starch, and softens the fibres of meats.

Hot water hardens and coagulates albumen, stops the flow of juices, and bursts the starch grains.

BOILING MEATS.

We cook meat in water for three purposes.

1. In cold water, to draw out the juice into the water, as soup, beef-tea.

2. In hot water, to keep the juices in the meat, as boiled meat.

3. In cold water, quickly heated, to have the juice partly in the meat and partly in the water, as in stews.

Long continued, slow boiling, softens the fibres of

tough meat, making them more digestible. The water in which they have been cooked should be used, as there is nutriment in it.

BOILED VEGETABLES.

Green vegetables should be well washed if at all wilted; lay in cold water for some time before cooking, then put into boiling, salted water, and cooked rapidly, uncovered, until tender.

New potatoes may be boiled as soon as pared, but in the late spring, old potatoes should stand an hour in cold water before cooking. Potatoes and cauliflower should be boiled slowly.

GRAINS.

All grains should be put into boiling, salted water, boiled rapidly ten minutes, then steamed, or simmer, until each grain is tender.

SIMMERING.

Much of our food is wasted by hard, rapid boiling. Albumen coagulates at 180°, but if put into boiling water, at 212°, it is toughened and made indigestible. When the nutriment is to be partly in the water, it is necessary to cook the food by simmering, instead of boiling. Bring the water to the boiling point, then add the food to be cooked, and keep the saucepan where the water will just bubble a little in one place.

All albuminous foods are best cooked in this way.

STEAMING.

There are two ways of cooking our food by steaming. One is by having a steamer, or covered pan, with holes in the bottom, placed over boiling water, the steam passing into the steamer and cooking the food; the other way is by having a smaller pan set into a larger pan, containing boiling water. The food is in the upper pan, and the heat from the lower pan passes through the upper pan, and cooks the food. All preparations of food that are likely to curdle, are best cooked in these two pans, which are called double boilers. You can manufacture one easily by using two different sized pans and putting a muffin ring, two or three nails, or any thing else you may think of, to keep the upper pan from resting on the bottom of the lower pan. In all cases the steam should be kept in by a tight cover, and the water should be replenished by adding *boiling* water from time to time. Never take the cover wholly off, as you allow cold air to enter, and if it is pudding or bread, it will fall and be heavy. Remove the cover a very little if you wish to look in, and cover immediately. *Never allow the water to stop boiling for a moment.*

ROASTING.

Roasting is to cook before an open fire, but most of the roast meat prepared in private families is cooked in the oven. The fire for roasting should be bright, free from ashes and sufficient to last through the entire baking. The oven should be very hot, 400°. Meat, poultry, game and fish should be wiped with a wet cloth, never washed, as water draws out the juices of the meat. Dredge with salt, pepper and flour. Salt draws out the juices, flour combines and forms a paste, and the intense heat makes a crust, which prevents the juices from escaping.

Never break this crust by sticking a fork or knife in, or you will let out the juices. Always place the meat on a rack to keep it from the fat. Put bits of suet on top of the meat and in the pan. If you have no suet use clarified drippings. Put no water in the pan, as it will produce steam in the oven and reduce the temperature to that of boiling water, 212°. Place in the hottest part of a very hot oven, let it bake for a few moments, this is to seal it, then, if in danger of burning, move to a cooler part of the oven. Baste often with the melted fat, and place a thin pan under the baking pan, to prevent the fat from burning. Dredge with flour once while baking.

Chickens and turkeys should be rubbed with soft butter, and some of the fat laid on top of them. You may cover any portion browning too quickly with oiled paper. After the outside is well seared, you may baste with a little butter dissolved in a little hot water, if they are not fat enough to baste with their own fat.

BROILING.

Broiling is cooking over bright-red coals. It is the most intense heat that we can get for cooking, and only the tender fibres of meat and fish are adapted to this way of cooking. The fire should be to the top of the fire box, bright red coals, with no blue flame, as this shows there is gas in the fuel. All the draughts should be open, that the smoke and gases may escape up the chimney. Have a large pan handy to hold the broiler over when you need to take it from the fire. Grease the broiler well with a piece of suet or salt pork. Do not salt, pepper, or flour the meat. Place the meat in the broiler with the thickest part nearest the handle. The fat edge of the meat should be nearest the handle also, if possible, so that as it melts it may run down and baste the meat. Too much fat will produce smoke, so it should be trimmed off. Cover the hand with a towel to moderate the heat. Hold the meat near the coals for a few seconds, turn at once and seal the other side. Frequent turning prevents burning, and keeps the juices in; it should be turned every ten seconds. Do not hold the meat in the smoke, but in the flame; and if there is a great deal of smoke, remove, and hold over the pan for a few moments. When done, place on a hot dish, sprinkle with salt and pepper, and serve immediately. Every thing else must be ready before this is started.

Chops and birds may be salted and peppered, and wrapped in buttered paper, and broiled in the papers. Glazed writing paper is the best, and it should be pinched around the edges to prevent the air from getting in, and the fat from getting out. They need a little more care, so as not to burn the paper, and take a little more time, but are very delicious.

PAN BROILING.

Sometimes, for various reasons, it is impossible to open the top of the fire to broil. Pan broiling is an excellent substitute, and if care be taken to remove all fat from the pan, so that the food may not be fried, it will be found a very satisfactory way of cooking. Heat a frying pan to a blue heat, grease slightly with a little suet, just enough to prevent the meat from sticking; put in the meat, and in ten seconds turn it, so as to seal the other side. Put the fork in the fat when turning it, so as not to let the juices out of the meat. When done, turn up on the fat edges, to cook the fat. Cook about four or five minutes, according to the thickness of the meat. As the fat melts drain off every drop, or it will be fried meat instead of broiled. Salt and pepper it when done, and serve on hot dish at once.

BRAISING.

Braising is a kind of stewing in a covered pan in the oven. It is an excellent way to prepare the tougher and less expensive cuts of meats, and if properly prepared the meat will be tender and palatable. The meat should be first salted, peppered, dredged with a little flour, and browned in a little fat; then put in a deep baking pan, and enough stock or water added to half cover the meat. This does not mean to use two pounds of meat and a pan that will hold a gallon of water. You may add any spices or vegetables that you desire. Keep the pan well covered and baste the meat frequently. The meat should cook slowly, and as the liquid evaporates do not add any more, but use the little left, as the foundation to make the gravy with.

FRYING.

Frying is cooking in deep, hot fat. There should always be enough fat to cover the article to be fried. The fat should be tested, and never used till hot enough to harden the outside of the article to be fried, and so protect the inside from absorbing the fat. A covering of eggs, or eggs in the material is often used, and the albumen of the egg hardens instantly, and prevents the fat from entering the food. Great care should be used to have the fat the proper heat. Do not put too many articles in at a time as they will chill the fat. Never have the material to be fried very cold. Do not have any steam or boiling water near the fat, and move carefully on the fire, for if it spills over it will take fire, and is very dangerous.

Cottolene is the best frying material; it is absolutely pure and wholesome, made of the cottonseed oil and beef drippings. As a substitute for butter and lard, for shortening, it is excellent, being much more economical, and produces very satisfactory results.

Lard should always be tried out before using, and one-fourth beef drippings to three-fourths lard is a very good proportion. Olive oil is too expensive for ordinary use.

TO PREPARE FAT FOR FRYING.

Cottolene is already prepared and need only be put in a *cold* pan and brought slowly to the proper heat. Care should be taken that it does not get too hot, as it does not sputter and bubble like lard.

Lard should be put on the fire and and when hot, a few slices of raw potato should be put in, and let remain till light brown, then taken out and thrown away. The potato has absorbent properties and draws out of the lard any unpleasant taste; it also attracts any floating particles and leaves the lard clear.

Keep the doors of the kitchen shut when frying

TEST OF FAT FOR FRYING.

When a small piece of bread browns in thirty seconds it is hot enough for potatoes and oysters. When it browns in forty seconds it is hot enough for material already cooked, such as fish balls, croquettes. When it browns in sixty seconds it is hot enough for material uncooked, such as doughnuts, fritters, fish, meat.

Test the fat always before frying anything. *Do not guess at it*, but take accurate time.

After frying one panful, allow the fat to heat again and test it every time before using.

If the fat is the right temperature you may fry anything and it will not taste; fish, then crullers, etc.

It is best to leave, if possible, all breaded articles till the last, as the crumbs drop off and burn in the fat, and may adhere to other material cooked.

All fried food should be drained on coarse, unglazed brown paper, which you can get at any meat market.

When you have finished using the fat, remove from the fire at once, let stand ten minutes to settle, then pour off slowly and carefully through a fine sieve, all but the sediment. Wipe the pan out with paper and save it for starting the fire in the morning. The fat may be used with care many times until it becomes very dark, when it is good only for soap grease.

SAUTÉING.

This is cooking in a little hot fat, browning first one side and then the other. But few articles are well prepared in this way, and although few will believe it, it is no more economical than plunging in deep fat, as the material absorbs more fat when all of the surface is not at once sealed by contact with the hot fat. Cold boiled potatoes, omelets, and fried cakes, are best prepared this way. The same rule holds good here of having the fat hot and the material not too cold.

LARDING.

Only lean, dry meat is improved by larding, such as fillet of beef, veal, grouse, quail. For larding use firm, solid, clear, fat, salt pork. Use only the part near the rind, not over an inch from the rind, as it becomes soft, and will trouble you by breaking. Cut into slices about an eighth of an inch thick, then into square strips; for beef, about the size of a lead pencil, for grouse or quails smaller. Push one of the strips or lardoons into the head of the needle, take up a stitch about an inch long with the point of the needle, draw the needle through, pushing the lard so that it will not come out of the needle. Leave the pork sticking out of the meat a third of an inch at each end. Put two or three rows of these lardoons, according to the size of the meat to be larded.

STIRRING, BEATING, FOLDING.

It is absolutely necessary, for the proper and successful preparation of most of the recipes containing well beaten eggs, that these three motions should be thoroughly understood. In many cases, the result of ignorance in this part of the preparation of food, results in heavy, leathery omelets, badly risen cake, and soggy, doughy muffins.

We *stir* in order to blend the material; this is done by keeping the spoon in the bowl and moving it round and round, having the bowl of the spoon touch the bottom of the dish and mash against the sides of the bowl.

We *beat* to entangle air in the mixture, such as beating eggs or batters. This is done by moving the spoon in a circle, scraping the bottom and sides of the bowl each time, bringing the spoon into the air and over into the opposite side of the dough. The bowl should be slightly tipped, and the spoon and bowl should be scraped, so that all the material will be well beaten.

We *fold* or *cut in* to avoid breaking the air cells, which we have made by thorough beating, as in the well beaten whites of eggs. This is done by turning the mixture over with the spoon, cutting through and folding over gently, but not *stirring* round and round. Stirring breaks the air cells, and all mixtures in which you have eggs used to raise the ingredients, should have a good beating just before baking, but do not, after you have beaten the mixture, stir it. Never stir or beat the mixture after folding in beaten whites or whipped cream.

BREAD CRUMBING.

Save all bits of bread that have been left over. Equal parts of crust and inside make the most appetizing color. Bakers bread is by far the best for this. Use no *burnt* or very dark-colored crusts. When dry and crisp, roll and sift through a fine sieve, and keep some constantly on hand, stored in a covered can or jar. When needed, season with a little salt and pepper, for every thing but sweet dishes. To roll in "crumbs, egg and crumbs," sprinkle a good layer on a board, break an egg into a saucer, beat up yolk and white slightly, add two tablespoonfuls cold water to one egg (this is to economise on the egg); lay the article to be breaded in the crumbs, cover all over with them, lift up, letting all drop off that will come, lay in the egg, dip the egg up over it till all is coated with the egg, breaking all the bubbles, as these will cause a croquette to break and run out, or become fat soaked; remove from the egg by dipping a broad bladed knife under carefully, lay in the crumbs again and toss them all over it. Be very careful in handling after they are crumbed the second time, as you may break through the egg, and it is the albumen of the egg that is to harden in the hot fat and seal the outside, that the food may not be greasy. Sift the crumbs after using and put away for future use. When forming cutlets or croquettes in a mold, grease the mold with a pastry brush, dipped in melted butter, fill with crumbs, toss them out, leaving in all that adhere to the mold, press the mixture into the mold, smooth off level with a knife, turn out on a well-crumbed board, cover with crumbs, then egg and crumbs again. Grease the mold but once.

BONING.

One object lesson is worth all the directions that can be given on boning. Have a small, sharp-pointed knife, and begin with something simple, such as a chop or steak first. Commence at the bone end, pushing the meat away from the bone without cutting the meat any more than possible. Always cut away from you.

Boned Leg of Lamb. Have the leg cut a little above the second joint, so that you will have a piece of flesh to fold over the hole that the bone leaves. Start at the large end, pushing the flesh away from the bone, and turning over like a glove. Cut close to the bone, but leave all gristle and cords on the bone. Salt and pepper the cavity and stuff; sew up the small end, fold the skin over the large end and sew up. A boned piece of meat takes much longer to cook than one with the bone in.

Boned Chicken. The fowl should not be drawn, and the skin should be firm and without a break. Cut off the head, leaving two inches of the neck on the body. Remove the pin feathers, singe, and wipe off gently. Make an incision from the back of the neck right down the middle of the back bone; scrape the meat away from the back bone until you feel the shoulder blade; scrape the flesh from this and follow it down to the bone. Be careful in going round the joints, as the skin lies very near the bone. Scrape on down the wing bone, turning the flesh away from the bone, that you may not cut the skin. Scrape carefully around the second joint of the wing, leaving the tips on, as it looks better when done. Do the other wing in the same way. Then work down towards the breast, removing the crop; keep close in to the breast bone, and when both sides of the bone are free, hold the flesh entirely away from the bone on both sides, and with great care cut the skin from the ridge. This is the most important part, that the fowl may look well when done. Separate the flesh from the ribs, holding the knife slanting, that you may not cut into the inside. Follow down the leg bone, going carefully round the joints. Separate the membrane at the end of the body without breaking, and cut the backbone just above the tail, leaving the tail on the boned portion. You will find left a perfect skeleton, with the entire contents untouched. Stuff, and sew up down the back, and skewer into shape.

CARE OF FOOD.

"Waste not; want not."

That the cost of living is very much increased by the wilful and ignorant waste in the kitchen, is an indisputable fact. The poor, as well as the rich, constantly throw away food which, if properly cared for, would make many a wholesome and palatable meal, without lightening a purse already too slender to meet the actual wants of the home. "Haste makes waste," and the hurry that throws out all the little odds and ends, will soon become a "habit, which is a cable; we weave a thread of it every day," and at last we cannot break it. Remember, that "Diligence is the mother of good luck," and nine-tenths of the good luck we see fall to other people, may be ours if we work for it. "A pound of pluck is worth a ton of luck." After each meal lay away all the remnants of food, and before marketing "take account of stock," that you may plan accordingly. As the principal causes of decomposition in our food are air, warmth, and moisture, it is important that these should be excluded. Keep all the perishable food in a cool, dry, enclosed place. As soon as the marketing comes home, remove at once from the papers, examine the meat and fish, lay on a plate and put away at once. Do not put fish in the same compartment with butter and milk, as it is apt to taste them. Look over the fruit and vegetables, remove any dried or spotted ones, and put immediately in a cold place. Wipe off the egg shells, so

CARE OF FOOD. 57

they may be ready for the coffee when used, and keep them in the ice box, as they keep fresh longer, and beat up much lighter and quicker if cold. Keep milk, cream and butter right against the ice. Fruit should be kept in a cool place, as it is more refreshing when cold. Examine fresh fruit and vegetables every day, remove the spotted ones, and if not too far spoiled cut well around the spots and stew the pieces. Never use any fruit that is decayed into the core or pit. Fry out all the odds and ends of fats at once, as they keep longer, and re-melt often. Do not keep milk in tin; bottles are best, if thoroughly scalded and aired. Lemons and cranberries may be kept for some time by covering them with cold water, keeping them under the water by some weight on them; change the water twice a week.

Keep nothing in paper as it is disorderly and draws vermin. Use boxes, bottles, or small tin cans with covers. Keep coffee and tea in airtight tin cans. Always put crackers in the oven a few moments before using; it makes them crisp. Keep the store room and refrigerator *perfectly* clean. Examine the refrigerator every day, that nothing may have dropped from the dishes and spoil. See that the drain pipe is kept free and the pan underneath well scoured out. Never put any hot food in the refrigerator.

SETTING THE TABLE.

A spotless, well laundried table-cloth, clear glasses, and well polished silver are the first necessities to an attractive table. No matter how inexpensive the appointments, a little pains can make the most humble table a source of delight and health to the entire household. It is of the utmost importance that our food should be served in an attractive way, as digestion begins before the food enters the mouth; the sight and desire, causing the flow of the first digestive fluid; and every woman should be glad to give the little time and few touches that can make so great a change in the comfort of a home. This, surely, is our sphere, and let each one of us do all we can, lovingly and willingly, remembering that the influence *must* pass on into other lives, and reach more than the loved ones in our own homes.

If possible, have a canton flannel or felt covering over the table, as it prevents noise, and the table-cloth lies smoother over it. Let the table-cloth be without wrinkles, always folding it in the creases, and keeping it laid flat when not used. Put the centre of the cloth in the centre of the table, the middle fold running straight. If there is a flower in the house always have it on the table for every meal; it should be placed in the centre of the table, on a centre cloth if desired. Knives and forks should be placed about seven inches apart, and about half an inch from the edge of the table; knives at the right, with the sharp edge turned towards the plate, and forks on the left with the tines up. Tumblers turned right side up in front of each plate, to the right, and butter plates beside them. Extra spoons outside of the knives in the order of the courses, having the first course spoon or fork outside. Napkins to the left of the fork, and at dinner a piece of bread or a roll in the fold. Plates laid right side up at each place between the knife and fork, or in a pile at the left hand side of the carver. Pepper and salt, if not individual, placed at the corners of the table. Jellies, salted nuts, pickles, and olives, in small dishes at uniform angles. Tablespoons, for serving, laid across each other at diagonal corners, or one in front of each dish to be served. Carving knife and fork on rests in front of the carver. Place the dishes on the table *straight*, directly in front of the one to serve them. Dishes for hot food should be heated. The last thing, think over the various dishes for the meal, and see that every thing needed for them is on the table, or a convenient side table. Arrange the chairs a little way from the table, straight in front of each place.

WAITING ON THE TABLE.

This should be done quietly, carefully and quickly. Noisy shoes, rustling skirts, should never be worn. In removing the covers from the dishes, turn them over quickly, so they may not drip, and lay on a side table. Cover the dishes as soon as they have been passed round the table. Stand on the left hand side of the one who is serving, and pass to each guest on the left hand side, taking care to have the serving spoon in a convenient position. Put each dish back in its proper place and keep the table, as far as possible, in order, till the end of the meal. Watch that the glasses are kept filled, three-quarters full only. In removing the plates lift up the plate with the knife and fork on it, watching that you may not let them drop off, then the small side dishes. Remove all but the flowers and brush off the crumbs before serving the dessert.

CLEARING THE TABLE.

Immediately after a meal remove all from the table, brush off the crumbs and fold the tablecloth, lifting it by taking hold of the middle fold half way towards the two ends, and raising the hands and drawing towards you. Lay lengthwise on the table, fold in the creases and put carefully away. Fold the under cover, lay away. Put the flowers back on the table, place the chairs back, brush up the crumbs with a whisp and dustpan. Darken the room.

WASHING DISHES.

"Beautiful hands are those that do
  Work that is earnest and brave and true,
  Moment for moment the whole day through."

We so often hear the remark that washing dishes ruins the hands, that perhaps a word in its favor from one who has spent many a pleasant hour at this homely task, may be helpful to those to whose lot it may fall to do this part of household work. In the first place, washing dishes does not injure the hands half as much as paring some fruits and vegetables, blacking stoves, scrubbing with inferior powders, and washing with strong solutions. If the dishes are well scraped and the grease removed, the hands well rinsed in clear cold water before drying, and then well dried, it will leave them soft and tender. It is the housework, not the washing dishes that causes such annoying results.

You need plenty of hot water, clean towels, a good dish cloth with no lint (an old flour bag hemmed is as nice as anything), and good soap. I can heartily recommend and always use Babbitt's. It is the best, most economical, softens the water, and injures the hands least.

Collect and scrape all the dishes, putting them near the sink; save every scrap of good food, even a crust of bread: "Wilful waste brings woeful want"; put away the pieces on *old* dishes. Fill all the pans that have had starchy food, such as grains, flour, corn starch, etc., with cold water, and stand away from the fire, as the heat will harden it. Put all the glasses together, and all the silver by itself. Rinse out the cups and pile up the saucers, small and large plates, rinse out the vegetable and meat dishes. Put the steel knives and forks together, and pile up all the tins. Burn up all meat and bones that cannot be used again, and there should be *none*, excepting from soup, as this is the food that will decompose quickly if allowed to remain in the garbage pail; open all the draughts when burning, and keep the lids on, and there will be no odor through the house. Save any fat from tried-out drippings; also rub out the greasy pans with paper and use this to kindle the fire in the morning. Fill the dish-pan two-thirds full of water as hot as you can bear your hand in, shake the soap around on a fork or in a shaker (never put it in the dish-pan as it wastes it and you will forget it and have it stick to the dishes). Lay in four or five tumblers, tipping them so as the water goes inside; wash quickly, lay upside down to drain, lay in four more and dry the others at once. If you work quickly there is no need of rinsing, they will be clean; but if you prefer, you can pour warm water over them. After the tumblers, the cups, a few at a time, taking care that there is no sugar left in them as that will make them sticky. Before drying each set, be sure and put more in the dish-pan as they will warm, and dry much quicker. Add hot water as the water cools, and put it in when there are no dishes in the pan, for fear of cracking them. When the water becomes at all greasy, rinse off the greasy dishes and get a fresh panful. Never put the silver in the pan and rattle it around as it scratches it. Wash it in hot soapy water and dry while hot and you will not need to clean it so often. Keep a little whiting in an old cup to rub off any discoloring from minerals. Never put steel knives in water as it melts the glue and causes the handles to come off. Clean the knives after every meal, and wipe with the back of the knife to the towel, not only to avoid cutting your hand but the towel also! Rinse out all greasy frying and roasting pans, with a little water from the dish-pan before washing. Wipe off Dover egg beaters as soon as used with a damp cloth; never put them in water. Rinse out the coffee and tea pot, but never put a soapy dish-cloth in either. Do not dry granite ware on the stove, as it chips the granite off. Do not throw refuse in the sink, and avoid letting the coffee grounds drain down, as they will close up the pipes. Wash out the sink and all around it with hot soap suds; wash out the towels with clean hot water and soap, rinse in cold water after each meal, drying in the sun as often as possible. Scrub up the tables and boards, rubbing with the grain of the wood. If care is used to let no grease into the sink, and if a kettle of boiling water in which has been dissolved a half cup of washing soda, is poured down the sink once a week, you will avoid the exasperating plumber, who spends a half day spread across your kitchen floor, blowing out your pipes, while the accompanying boy puts out your fire!

SOUP.

During the greater part of the year there is nothing that helps a housekeeper more in serving satisfactory dinners than a little good soup. With care and economy some kind may always be ready for each day. In marketing, see that all the bones and trimmings cut off from the meat are sent home, and always boil them up, with or without any bones and scraps of meat you may have saved, using a few vegetables, and when done put away for stock. Have a vessel for keeping the bones left over from meals, and after laying aside any meat that can be made up in other ways, throw all the scraps, gristle, and any gravy that may not be needed for warming up, into the vessel with the bones. Keep mixed herbs and spices always in the house, and one carrot, onion, turnip and a little parsley at hand. Do not buy but one or two carrots or onions at a time, as they spoil rapidly. Save all the green stalks of celery not fit to serve at the table, also any little bits of green vegetables, such as peas, beans, etc.; rinse off in hot water and keep for serving in soup; and try and remember to do it before they spoil! Do not throw away one chop bone, but put it in a cold place and you will soon find another to keep it company! Save the water in which meat, such as tongue, lamb, poultry, veal, has been boiled and use it for making soup.

As soup needs hours for cooking, plan to make the

stock for it on the days when you use the fire and make the quickly-prepared soups the days that the fire is not needed. "A penny saved is a penny earned" and if she be wise, by watchfulness, the housekeeper can earn as much as the bread-winner.

STOCK.

Stock, as the word implies, is something that has been prepared and is ready for use at any time the demand may be made for it, which is very often, if many palatable sauces are used. It is prepared by cooking bones, meat and vegetables in water, till all the juice has been extracted, and then strained and put away. Vegetables sour quickly, so if the stock is to be kept some little time, it is best not to use them. It keeps longer when the fat on the top is not broken, and bringing to a boil every day keeps it from spoiling as quickly. It is better to make it in small quantities, than to risk keeping it over three days, unless the weather is very cold. You may use as many, or as few of the ingredients called for as you please, and bits of egg or apples may be added.

White stock is made with veal or poultry.

In cooking the stock, the meat and bones should always be soaked for an hour in cold water, to draw out the juice, then brought slowly to a boil, and simmered until the meat is in shreds, seven to eight hours. Never skim the top of the water as the soup boils, and the particles rise, for it is the albumen of the meat, and if the meat and bones have been wiped and the pot and water are clean, why take out and throw away what you want in the soup? Keep the kettle closely covered, that the flavor may be kept, and the stock not boil away in steam. If possible prepare the day before, that it may stand till the fat is hard. You may use any combination of mutton, veal, poultry or beef, as you have them, but when purchasing meat for stock, buy the kind stated in the recipe. The meat and vegetables that have been used for making the stock are worthless; and as all the nutriment has been drawn out by long continued cooking they can only be thrown away. Always have some fat in the stock; it melts, and when cold will serve to seal it and keep it from spoiling. The herbs and spices should always be whole, and the vegetables, meat and bones in small pieces. Some of the meats should always be broiled, roasted, or fried, before using for soup, as the peculiar flavor developed in that kind of cooking is called osmazome, and is needed in soup. If you have no pieces of roasted, broiled or fried meat, dredge half the raw meat with salt, pepper and flour, and fry in some of the fat till brown. Rinse out the frying pan with hot water, that you may get all the brown off it, and add to the soup.

TO CLARIFY SOUP.

The stock should be made the day before, and if it cannot be, you can remove the fat by skimming off with a spoon, and laying brown paper on the top to absorb the remainder of the fat. You cannot clarify hot stock. Allow the fat to harden over night, then it can be removed in a cake from the top; and wipe the edges of the bowl and the top of the stock with a bit of cheese cloth dipped in hot water. Every particle of fat must be removed at this time, as it will float when the soup is served. Add to the cold stock the whites and shells of raw eggs, allowing one egg for one quart of stock; beat well, set over the fire and bring to a boil slowly; simmer 20 minutes without stirring. Wring a napkin out of hot water, put it over a coarse sieve, then a fine strainer over the napkin to catch the shells and egg. Let it drain through this, but do not squeeze the napkin. The stock is then ready to use for any clear soup and should be brought to the boiling point, and anything added to it that you desire.

Clear soups are not as nutritious as others, and for family use a soup should never be clarified.

Pureés and thick soups should always have the flour and butter cooked together, and the liquid added gradually, that the ingredients may not separate, as one sometimes sees in pea soup, when the peas and water are very distinct.

SOUP STOCK.

1 lb. marrow bone,
2 qts. cold water,
1 sprig thyme,
1 " majoram,
1 " summer savory,
1 " sage,
1 " parsley,
1 " celery,
1 lb. shin beef,
6 whole cloves,
6 peppercorns,
2 tsp. salt,
1 small onion,
$\frac{1}{2}$ " carrot,
$\frac{1}{2}$ " turnip,
$\frac{1}{2}$ leaf cabbage.

Wipe and cut the meat and bones into small pieces. Put bones, half the meat, water, spices and herbs into the kettle. Let stand half an hour. Dredge the rest of the meat with pepper, salt, flour, and fry till brown in a little hot drippings. Put the fried meat into the kettle, fry the vegetables (cut fine), put them into the kettle. Bring to a boil slowly; boil 10 minutes; do not skim; simmer 6 or 7 hours and strain. Set aside till cold; when needed for soup, remove the fat, heat and season to taste.

LEFT-OVER SOUP.

Put in a kettle any bones that have been left from roast beef, steak, or chops, any pieces of meat cut fine, cover with cold water. To 2 qts. of water add the same seasoning as for soup stock. Simmer till the meat is in shreds, strain, when cold remove the fat. Bring to the boiling point and add any small pieces of cooked vegetables that have been left over, as peas, beans, tomatoes, turnips, potatoes or rice.

MACARONI SOUP.

Break the macaroni into half-inch pieces, cook in boiling salted water about half an hour. Drain the macaroni and add to boiling stock, allowing 1 c. macaroni to 1 qt. stock. Season with salt and pepper.

VEGETABLE SOUP.

1 qt. stock, $\frac{1}{3}$ c. carrot, $\frac{1}{3}$ c. turnip, $\frac{1}{3}$ c. potato, $\frac{1}{4}$ c. celery.

Wash and pare the turnip and potato, scrape the carrot and celery. Cut into quarter-inch dice and cook in boiling salted water till tender. Drain and add to the boiling stock. Season with salt and pepper.

TOMATO SOUP.

1 qt. tomatoes.	2 whole cloves.
1 pt. stock.	1 tsp. salt.
2 tbsp. flour.	$\frac{1}{2}$ " sugar.
3 " butter.	1 sprig parsley.
2 peppercorns.	$\frac{1}{2}$ onion.

Boil the tomatoes, stock and seasoning ten minutes. Cook the butter and flour till smooth and frothy, add the soup gradually. Strain through a fine sieve. Season with salt and pepper. You may use water if you have not stock.

SPLIT PEA SOUP.

$\frac{1}{2}$ c. dried split peas.	$\frac{1}{2}$ tsp. sugar.
3 c. cold water.	$\frac{1}{2}$ " salt.
$\frac{1}{2}$ tbsp. butter.	1 ssp. white pepper.
$\frac{1}{2}$ " flour.	Milk.
1 stalk celery.	1 sprig parsley.
1 slice onion.	

Pick over and wash the peas. Soak in the cold water 2 h. Put on the fire, add the onion, celery and parsley, and simmer 2 h. Mash through a fine strainer, return to the fire. Cook the flour and the butter till smooth, add the strained soup gradually, then the milk and seasoning. It may be made without soaking the peas.

POTATO SOUP.

3 medium sized potatoes.	$\frac{1}{2}$ ssp. white pepper.
1$\frac{1}{2}$ c. milk.	$\frac{1}{2}$ tbsp. flour.
1$\frac{1}{2}$ c. hot water.	$\frac{1}{2}$ " butter.
1 tsp. chopped onion.	1 stalk celery.
1 " salt.	1 sprig parsley.

Wash, pare and cook the potatoes till soft. Cook the milk, water, parsley, celery and onion in a double boiler 15 m. When the potatoes are done, drain and mash, add the hot milk gradually; cook the butter and flour till smooth and frothy, add the hot soup slowly, stirring constantly, then the salt and pepper.

MOCK BISQUE.

1 pt. tomato.	1 tbsp. butter.
1 pt. milk.	2 tsp. cornstarch.
½ small onion. ½ tsp. soda.	1 bay leaf.

Boil the tomato, onion and bay leaf 15 m., add the soda, boil 5 m. longer; heat the milk; cook the flour and cornstarch till smooth and frothy, add the tomato slowly, stirring well. Mash through a fine strainer and add to the hot milk. Add salt and pepper to taste and serve at once. Do not boil after adding the milk. You may add 1 c. whipped cream just before serving.

CONSOMMÉ.

2 lbs. shin beef.	4 qts. cold water.
2 " marrow bone.	2 oz. lean ham.
4 " knuckle of veal.	6 cloves.
1 tbsp. salt.	6 peppercorns.
3 " chopped onion.	1 sprig parsley.
3 " " carrot.	1 " thyme.
3 " " turnip.	1 " summer savory.
3 " " celery.	2 bay leaves.
4 " " suet.	1 sage leaf.
5 allspice berries.	1 in. stick cinnamon.
White and shells of 2 eggs.	1 blade mace.
1 ssp. celery seed.	Rind and juice 1 lemon.

Proceed as for soup stock, using the suet to fry the meat, vegetables and ham in. When cold, remove every particle of fat, beat the whites of the eggs light, add them to the stock with the rind and juice of the lemon and the celery seed; bring slowly to the boiling point, then let it simmer for $\frac{1}{2}$ h. Strain through a napkin dipped in hot water.

BOUILLON.

4 lbs. clear beef from the round. Whites 2 eggs.
2 qts. cold water. 6 peppercorns.
2 tbsp. onion. 3 cloves.
2 " turnip. 1 in. stick cinnamon.
2 " celery. 1½ tbsp. salt.
1 bay leaf. 1 sprig parsley.
1 sage leaf. 1 " thyme.
  1 sprig summer savory.

Proceed the same as for Consommé.

JULIENNE SOUP.

1 qt. clear stock. ½ c. celery.
½ c. carrot. ½ c. lettuce.
½ c. turnip. ½ c. peas.

Cut the vegetables into fine, thin strips, and cook in boiling, salted water, till tender. Shred the lettuce very fine and cook in boiling water 10 m. Drain the vegetables and the lettuce and add to the hot stock. Season if necessary.

CREAM OF ASPARAGUS.

1 can asparagus. 2 tbsp. butter.
1 pt. white stock. 1 " onion.
1 " cream or milk. 2 " flour.
⅛ tsp. white pepper. 1 tsp. sugar.
  1½ tsp salt.

Cut off the heads of asparagus. Cut up stalks, simmer in the stock ½ h. Fry the onion in the butter till yellow, add the flour, add the stock slowly, simmer 10 m. Put through a fine sieve, add cream, salt, pepper, sugar, and when nearly boiling add heads of asparagus. Do not boil after adding the cream or it will curdle.

VELVET SOUP.

⅔ qt. chicken stock.	1 stalk celery.
⅞ c. large white bread crumbs.	1 blade mace.
1 clove.	½ in. stick cinnamon.
1 bay leaf.	1 slice carrot.
1 sprig parsley.	⅓ onion.
⅓ c. almonds.	½ tbsp. salt.
⅓ c. chicken breast.	1½ c. cream.
1 tbsp. flour.	1 tbsp. butter.

Cook stock, crumbs, celery, mace, cinnamon, bay leaf, parsley, onion, carrot, and salt 1 h. Pound the chicken breast and almonds to a paste, add to the stock, cook 5 m. Mash through a fine sieve, add the hot cream. Cook the flour and butter, add the stock slowly, stirring well; season with pepper and salt if needed.

OYSTER SOUP.

1 qt. oysters.	2 tbsp. cornstarch.
1 pt. milk (hot).	1 ssp. white pepper.
1 tbsp. butter.	1 small blade mace.

Wash the oysters in 1 c. cold water; add this to the oyster liquor and strain; put the liquor and the mace on to boil. Remove the scum, add the oysters, cook about two minutes, until they are ruffled and

SOUP.

plump. Cook the flour and cornstarch till smooth and frothy, add the hot milk slowly, stirring hard; boil 5 m., add the oysters, salt if needed. Remove the mace and serve at once.

CLAM SOUP.

25 clams.	2 tbsp. butter.
1 pt. milk, scalded.	1 dozen crackers.
1 pt. water.	1 inch blade of mace.
Salt and pepper.	½ tbsp. flour.

Drain the clams and put the liquor on to boil with the mace; chop the clams. Skim the liquor as it boils; when it has boiled 5 m. add the clams and water and boil 5 m. Cook the flour in the butter, add the milk gradually, stirring well; remove the mace, add the clams to the milk, but do not let it boil, or it will curdle. Season with salt and pepper and serve at once.

CLAM CHOWDER.

25 clams.	3 water biscuits.
½ lb. veal.	½ tsp. ea. thyme and majoram.
¼ lb. bacon.	½ tsp. chopped parsley.
2 potatoes.	1 c. stewed tomatoes.
1 c. water.	½ tbsp. flour.
1 c. milk.	½ " butter.

Cut the bacon, veal and potatoes into dice. Chop the onion fine. If the clams are small leave them whole, but if large cut in pieces. Put the bacon in the pot first, a sprinkling of herbs, a little salt and pepper, then veal, tomato and clams. Continue till all is used. Add the boiling water, cover, and simmer 30 m. Heat the milk, cook the butter and flour till smooth, add the hot milk gradually, stirring well; then stir this into the clams, break up the crackers and season with salt and pepper and serve at once. Do not boil after adding the milk.

BISQUE OF LOBSTER.

2½ lbs. lobster with coral.	1 c. stale white br'd crumbs.
¾ pt. white stock.	½ tbsp. salt.
1 pt. cream.	½ " flour.
1 stalk celery.	1½ " butter.
1 small slice onion.	1 sprig parsley.
1 " blade mace.	1 bay leaf.
1 spk. nutmeg.	¼ tsp. white pepper.
½ c. bits of meat from the claws.	

Chop the meat fine as meal, put into a saucepan with half the stock; pound the lobster coral with ½ the butter, add this to the stock; tie the onion, mace, parsley and bay leaf in a small bag, add to the stock and simmer 1 h. Put the rest of the stock and the bread in a double boiler, simmer ½ h. Scald the cream. Strain all the stock through a fine sieve, cook the other half of the flour and butter till smooth, add the strained mixture and the seasoning, strain, add the cream and bits of meat. Do not boil after the cream is added.

PURÉE OF SALMON.

1 pt. milk.	1 sprig parsley.
1 slice onion.	½ tsp. salt.
½ tbsp. butter.	⅛ " white pepper.
½ " flour.	1 spk. cayenne.
½ c. cooked salmon.	1 " nutmeg.

Cook the milk, onion and parsley in a double boiler 10 m. Free the salmon from oil and bones and flake it. Cook butter and flour till smooth and frothy, add milk gradually, stirring well, then salmon, seasoning, strain and serve. Do not boil after the salmon is added.

FISH.

Fish is a wholesome, valuable article of food. It contains a large amount of nitrogeneous material and is rich in phosphorus.

The red-blooded fish, such as salmon, bluefish, mackerel, are the richest, and have the oil distributed through the body, and are therefore more indigestible, and should never be given to invalids or persons of weak digestion.

The white varieties, such as cod, halibut, flounder, have the oil stored in the liver, as cod liver oil, and are more easily digested, but should be served or cooked with some kind of fat to be palatable. Sauces will contain the palatable proportions needed.

Fish should always be perfectly fresh and well cooked or it is unfit to eat. Fresh fish will have the flesh firm and hard, the eyes full and rounded, the gills red. Do not buy any other. It should be cleaned at once, wiped out with a damp cloth and never salted until just before cooking, or you will draw out the juices. Lay in a cold place till needed, but do not let the ice touch it, and put it away from the butter or milk. Good fishermen say that fresh water fish should be cooked as soon as they come from the water, but salt water fish are improved by keeping a few hours before cooking. Fillets of fish are long, thin slices, or pieces of flesh with no bones. Flat fish, like flounder, make the best fillets, although you can cut other fish into thin slices. Frozen fish should be laid in cold water till thawed.

FISH.

TO CLEAN A FISH.

Remove the scales before opening, scraping with a knife from the tail towards the head. Sprinkle the hand with a little salt and the fish will not slip. Work slowly, so that the scales may not fly, and dip the knife often in cold water. Do not cut off the head and tail if the fish is to be served whole. Cut on the under side, from the gills down, making an opening only large enough to remove the entrails; remove all the blood and wipe out with a damp cloth. Rub the inside with salt just before cooking.

BAKED FISH. (Whole.)

Do not cut off the head or tail. Remove the scales by scraping with a small, sharp knife, beginning at the tail and going towards the head. Cut off the fins with a pair of scissors. Make an incision from the gills, half way down the lower part of the body; remove the entrails and scrape out the blood and white part adhering to the back bone. Wipe out with a cloth wet in salt water and dry thoroughly. Sprinkle the inside with salt, stuff and sew up with coarse darning cotton. Cut gashes two inches apart on each side. Wind a little cotton around the head that the stuffing may not come out. Dredge with salt, pepper and flour. Rub the baking pan with fat salt pork and put small pieces under and over the fish. You may skewer it like a letter S, or a circle. Bake in a hot oven with no water in the pan; baste every 10 m. When done, remove the fish to a hot platter, using a pancake turner to lift it with; lift the head a little to draw out the cotton, untie the head and remove the skewers. Make a bed of parsley round it, decorate with fancy pieces of lemon.

STUFFING FOR BAKED FISH. (5 lbs.)

1 c. cracker or bread crumbs. 1 tsp. chopped parsley.
1 ssp. salt.   1 "   "   onion.
1 " pepper.   1 "   "   pickles.
¼ c. melted butter.   ½ "   lemon juice.

If you prefer a moist stuffing wet with a little cold water.

BOILED FISH.

Wipe the fish and tie up in a cloth. Put 1 tbsp. salt into a pot of boiling water, put the fish in on a plate, let simmer till done.

BROILED FISH.

Fish weighing from ¾ lb. to 4 lb. are the best for broiling. Split the larger ones down the back and remove the back bone, head and tail. Sprinkle with salt and pepper; rub dry fish with soft butter. Grease the double broiler with fat salt pork. Put the thickest part of the fish in the middle of the broiler and broil the flesh side first. The thickness of the fish must be the guide as to time. Turn every 10 s. and serve on hot platter.

FRIED FISH.

Small fish, such as smelts, weak fish, porgies, etc., are best fried; also, slices of cod, halibut, haddock. Do not remove the heads and tails from the small fish. Clean, wipe and dry the fish, dredge with salt and pepper, roll in fine sifted bread crumbs, egg and

FISH. 79

crumbs, and sauté in frying pan with a little cottolene, browning first one side and then the other, or plunge in deep, hot cottolene.

FISH BALLS.

1 c. raw salt fish.	1 egg, well beaten.
2 c. raw potatoes.	¼ ssp. white pepper.
1 tsp. butter.	spk. cayenne.
Salt, if needed.	Dash of nutmeg.

Shred the fish. Pare and quarter the potatoes. Cook the fish and potatoes in boiling water till the potatoes are done. Drain very dry; mash and beat the fish and potatoes till very light, add the butter and seasoning; beat well; add the egg. Drop a few at a time into hot cottolene.

FRIED SMELTS.

Clean them by pressing out the contents through an opening under the gills. Wash quickly, dry thoroughly; dredge with salt and pepper. Make them into circles by putting the tail through the eyes, or run two wooden toothpicks through two or three, having the heads all one way. Cover with bread crumbs, egg and crumbs, and fry in hot cottolene. Serve on the skewers with tartar sauce.

FRIED CODFISH.

Cut into small pieces for serving, skewering the little bits into shape; salt and pepper each piece on both sides, squeeze a few drops of lemon on each piece, roll in fine bread crumbs, egg and crumbs, and fry in hot cottolene. Serve with tartar or Worcestershire sauce.

CREAMED OR PICKED UP SALT FISH.

Shred the fish and put on in cold water, boil slowly 20 m.; drain, taste it, and if too salt put on in cold water again and bring to a boil, and throw off that water. This may be done hours before, using 2 c. white sauce, 1 c. cooked fish, 1 c. cold boiled potato cubes, 1 ssp. white pepper, 1 tbsp. chopped parsley, 1 hard boiled egg. Make the sauce, add the fish, beat well, add the potato, stir carefully; serve on rounds of toast, decorated with the parsley and chopped egg.

SCALLOPED FISH.

Any remnants of cold, boiled or baked fish. Pick into small pieces, season with salt and pepper, and 1 tsp. lemon juice to 1 c. fish. Put into a shallow baking dish a layer of fish, then a little stuffing (if you have any left), then a layer of sauce. You can use white sauce if you have none left over. Cover with coarse white bread crumbs, seasoned with a shake of salt and pepper and 1 tbsp, of melted butter to 1 c. crumbs. Toss them with a fork as you pour the butter over them. Bake in the oven till crumbs are brown.

FISH AU GRATIN.

Skin the fish, cut off head, tail; split down the back, remove the back bone. Put on a buttered baking sheet that will fit loosely in a large baking pan. Season with salt and pepper. Prepare the sauce as follows: 1 pt. stock, 2 tbsp. flour, 2 tbsp. butter, 1 tbsp. minced onion, 1 tbsp. chopped pickles, 1 tbsp. chopped capers, 1 tbsp. lemon juice, 1 tbsp. chopped olives, 1 tbsp. chopped parsley, $\frac{1}{2}$ tsp. salt,

FISH. 81

⅛ ssp. pepper. Heat the stock, cook the onion in the butter till light yellow, add the dry flour, then the hot stock slowly, beating hard, then the salt, pepper, and lemon juice, lastly the chopped ingredients. Cover the fish with the sauce, cover all with buttered bread crumbs (1 tbsp. melted butter to 1 c. crumbs), and bake about 25 m., taking care not to have the crumbs too brown.

FISH AU GRATIN NO. 2.

Flake any cold cooked fish, put a layer on a platter, cover with white sauce, then another layer of fish and sauce. Cover the top with buttered crumbs. Bake till the crumbs are delicate brown.

BLANQUETTE OF SALMON.

½ can or ½ lb. of cold boiled salmon, 1 c. white sauce, 1 tsp. lemon juice, spk. cayenne, ⅛ tsp. onion juice. Free the salmon from oil and bones, pick very fine; put into the white sauce with the seasoning, serve hot in potato border, or in shells covered with buttered bread crumbs and browned in the oven.

FISH SOUFFLÉ.

Make the same as fish balls; use the yolks of two eggs well beaten, lastly the whites, beaten stiff and cut in lightly. Bake in a buttered dish 20 m.

TURBAN OF FLOUNDER.

4 fillets of flounder. 1 egg.
2 tbsp. butter. 2 tbsp. chopped parsley.
Discs of cold boiled beets. Bread crumbs.

Salt and pepper each fillet, dip in the melted butter, roll up and fasten with a wooden toothpick. Dip in crumbs, egg and crumbs, and fry in hot cottolene. Arrange in a circle on a platter, place a disc of beet on the top of each turban, and sprinkle with chopped parsley. Serve with Romoulade sauce in the centre of the dish.

TURBANS OF FISH WITH OYSTERS.

4 fillets of flounder.	1 tsp. salt.
12 oysters.	3 tbsp. butter.
1 pt. fine bread crumbs.	$\frac{1}{3}$ tsp. cayenne.
1 spk. nutmeg.	1 tsp. chopped parsley.
Yolks 2 eggs.	1 tbsp. lemon juice.

Drain and chop the oysters very fine, add the crumbs, seasoning, butter, and pound to a paste; add the yolks, and if needed, two tablespoonfuls of oyster liquor. It should now be a paste moist enough to spread. Salt and pepper the fillets, spread with the paste, roll up, fasten with a wooden toothpick, roll and spread again with the mixture, then in crumbs, egg and crumbs, and fry in hot cottolene. Serve with Bechamel sauce.

OYSTER BALLS.

12 oysters.	1 tbsp. lemon juice.
2 c. fine bread crumbs.	3 " butter, melted.
1 spk. nutmeg.	1 tsp. salt.
Yolks 2 eggs.	1 " chopped parsley.
$\frac{1}{3}$ tsp. cayenne.	

Drain the oysters and chop very fine. Add the eggs and enough oyster liquor to form into balls. Roll the balls in crumbs, egg and crumbs, and fry in hot cottolene.

SALMON TIMBALES.

¾ lb. salmon, canned.
3 tbsp. butter.
1½ tsp. salt.
¼ " pepper.
½ c. white bread crumbs.
1 c. cream.
Spk. nutmeg.
3 eggs, beaten separately.

Free the salmon from oil and bones and shred it very fine. Cook the bread and cream in the double boiler fifteen minutes, add the butter, stir well, then the salmon, then the yolks, seasoning, and mushrooms. Beat the whites stiff and beat them in gently. Put in buttered timbale molds stood in a pan of hot water, bake three-quarters of an hour. Cover them while baking with buttered paper. Serve with lobster sauce. These are very delicious.

SHELL FISH.

OYSTERS.

Oysters are mostly composed of water, contain but little nutriment in proportion to the cost. They are easily digested when slightly cooked, but are tough and very unwholesome when overdone. They are mostly used as a relish for an invalid rather than a nutritious food. During the summer they are soft and unhealthy, and should be eaten only in the cooler months.

TO PREPARE OYSTERS FOR COOKING.

Wash the oysters separately by dipping quickly into cold water, passing the fingers over them that there may be no shell. If for frying or broiling, season with a little salt and pepper and let stand 15 m. before cooking.

RAW OYSTERS.

The small, fat Blue Points are the best for serving raw. They should be kept on ice till ready to serve. Open the shells just before serving, remove half the shell and detach the oyster from the other half. Season with a very little salt and pepper and serve with pieces of lemon. You can hollow out a cavity in a block of ice by using hot irons; lay a few ferns and bright flowers on the sides of the cavity and put the oysters in. The ice may be laid in a napkin on a large platter and the base surrounded by flowers and ferns.

FRIED OYSTERS.

Dip prepared oysters in crumbs, egg and crumbs, and fry in hot cottolene. Serve with lemon.

BROILED OYSTERS.

Prepare the oysters, dip in melted butter, put in a fine greased broiler and broil till plump and the juice flows.

CREAMED OYSTERS.

1 pt. oysters, 1 pt. milk or cream, 2 tbsp. butter, 2 tbsp. flour, ½ tsp. salt, ½ ssp. white pepper, 1 blade mace, 1 slice onion, 1 ssp. celery salt, spk. cayenne. Heat the milk with the onion and mace, cook the flour and butter till smooth and frothy; remove the mace and onion from the milk, add the milk slowly, stirring hard, then the seasoning. Cook the oysters in their own liquor, drain, and add to the sauce. Add more salt and pepper if needed.

FRICASSEED OYSTERS.

Cook 1 pt. of oysters in hot butter till plump. Drain and keep the oysters hot. Measure the liquor left after cooking them in the butter, and add enough cream or milk to this to make 1 c. in all. Cook 1 tbsp. flour in 1 tbsp. butter, add the hot cream slowly. Season with 1 tsp. lemon juice, salt and pepper to taste, and spk. cayenne. Add 1 well-beaten egg, 1 tbsp. chopped parsley, and the oysters. Heat 1 m., serve on toast or in patty cases.

SCALLOPED OYSTERS.

Put into a buttered baking dish a layer of buttered cracker crumbs, allowing 1 tbsp. melted butter to

1 c. crumbs, then a layer of oysters; sprinkle with a little salt, pepper and a very little mace, then another layer of crumbs, then oysters, and last crumbs. Bake about 20 m. in a hot oven.

HUITRE A LA DAUPHINE.

Prepare the oysters for frying. Make 1 c. hot tomato sauce, and small pieces of toast. Fry the oysters, lay on the toast, and pour the sauce over them. Serve at once. Or you may pour the sauce around them.

LITTLE PIGS IN BLANKETS.

Prepare the oysters and season with salt, pepper and a few drops of lemon juice. Wrap each oyster in a very thin slice of bacon just large enough to cover, skewer up with $\frac{1}{2}$ wooden toothpick, fry in hot pan with no fat, till the bacon is crisp. Serve on toast.

LOBSTER.

It is best to buy the lobster alive, and cook it yourself; then there is no doubt that it is freshly boiled. It should be boiled within eighteen hours of using. If purchased already cooked, draw back the tail; if it springs into position again, it is safe to think the fish is good.

TO SELECT A LOBSTER.

Choose one of medium size, heavy in proportion, hard, solid shell streaked with black.

TO BOIL A LOBSTER.

Have a pot of boiling water with 1 tbsp. salt in it, plunge the lobster in head first. This kills it instant-

SHELL FISH. 87

ly and is less cruel than to put in cold water and bring to a boil. Boil 20 m. If boiled longer it toughens the meat. Remove at once from the water and set aside to cool.

TO OPEN A LOBSTER.

Break off all the claws, separate the tail from the body, remove the body from the shell, saving the green liver and the coral. Cut very carefully the thin shell on the under part of the tail, bend open slightly and remove the meat in one piece by taking a firm hold at the larger end of the tail and drawing it out. Separate this meat carefully down the middle and you will find a very thin vein running the entire length. Remove this without breaking, as it is the intestinal canal. This is sometimes dark colored and sometimes the color of the meat. Split the body and pick out the bits of meat, rejecting the spongy substances. Hammer the shells of the large claws on the edge, and remove the meat. Pick out all the bits of meat from the small claws. Clean and wash the shells and save a few of the small claws for garnishing.

CREAMED LOBSTER.

Allow 1 c. lobster meat to 1 c. white or cream sauce. Make the sauce, add the lobster meat, add 1 tsp. lemon juice, spk. cayenne.

DEVILED LOBSTER.

Season 1 c. lobster meat cut fine, with salt, pepper, mustard, cayenne, onion juice, chopped parsley and Worcestershire sauce. Mix with $\frac{1}{2}$ c. cream sauce. Put into the shell, cover with $\frac{1}{2}$ c. cracker crumbs moistened with 1 tbsp. melted butter. Bake about 15 m.

LOBSTER CUTLETS OR CROQUETTES.

1 pt. lobster meat minced very fine, 1 c. thick cream sauce, 1 ssp. mustard, few drops onion juice, 1 tsp. lemon juice, spk. cayenne. Make the sauce, add the meat and seasoning; beat well, spread out on a buttered platter 1 in. thick. When cool, shape into croquettes or cut into cutlets. If you have a cutlet mold, butter the mold, sprinkle with crumbs, press the lobster in, turn out on a well crumbed board, lay in egg and crumbs and fry. Put part of a small claw in small end of each. Roll the croquettes in crumbs, egg and crumbs, and fry in hot cottolene.

SCALLOPS.

Only the muscular part which unites the shell is eaten. They may be stewed like oysters or fried.

FRIED SCALLOPS.

Sprinkle with salt and pepper, roll in crumbs, egg and crumbs, and fry in hot cottolene. They are delicious served with Mayonnaise.

CRABS.

Crabs, like lobsters, are only fit to use when cooked alive. Choose the heavy medium-sized ones. When the crab loses its shell it is called a soft-shell crab, and as the shell forms in three days they are scarce and expensive.

TO BOIL CRABS.

Put head first into boiling salted water and boil 15 m. Remove the outside shell and the spongy substance, taking care that the under part is free from sand. Serve them in the shells.

SOFT SHELL CRABS.

They should be alive and freshly caught. Remove the sand bags and spongy substance, wash and dry thoroughly; season with salt and pepper and dip in seasoned crumbs, egg and crumbs, and fry in hot cottolene.

DEVILED CRABS.

Boil the crabs 15 m. Pick the meat from the shells, taking care not to use the spongy substance or the stomach, which lies in the head. Mince the meat very fine, and to one cup of meat add one cup of thick cream sauce for croquettes. Beat thoroughly and season highly with cayenne, mustard and lemon juice. Fill the shells, cover with buttered crumbs, bake 10 m.

BROILED CRABS.

Clean the crabs, season with salt and cayenne, boil one minute. Take up and broil over a hot fire eight to ten minutes.

MEAT.

Beef, mutton, lamb, veal, and pork are classed under this head, and with regard to their nutritive qualities stand in the above order.

BEEF.

Good beef should have firm, fine grained flesh, yellowish white fat, and when first cut should be dark red, changing to bright red in a few moments, and have a juicy appearance. The suet should be dry and crumble easily. The most expensive pieces of beef are from the ribs, sirloin, rump, and round. These cuts contain the most tender fibres of the meat, and are best adapted to rapid cooking, such as roasting and broiling. Cheaper cuts come from the shoulder, neck, flank, brisket and shin, and as the fibres are tougher they require slow and long continued cooking, by which the fibres are softened, the meat made tender and nutritious, and the juices drawn out. Wherever there is motion the juices flow; consequently we find the neck a very juicy part, while the tenderloin being a little cushion on which the ribs rest, and free from motion, has very little juice. Around the tail, where the rump and round lie, and the shin, which is near the foot, the meat is juicy; the rump and round tender; the shin meat tough, but containing a great deal of juice that can be drawn out into soups. Remove from the paper as soon as it comes, as it draws out the juices.

MEAT.   91

ROAST BEEF.

Wipe with a wet cloth, lay the meat on a rack in the pan, dredge all over with salt, pepper and flour. Put small pieces of suet on top of the meat and in the pan. Place in the hottest part of a hot oven 10 minutes. Do not put any water in the pan at first, as it reduces the temperature, and you want to set the outside of the meat so that the juices may be in the meat. Salt draws out the juices, the flour makes a paste, and the heat forms a crust. Never pierce the crust with a fork but turn and lift with a spoon carefully. After 10 m. reduce the heat if it is likely to burn, and if on the bottom of the oven, place a pan under, that the fat may not burn. Baste often, and if necessary you may add a little hot water, but basting with the fat gives the most delicious roast. Dredge with flour and salt once during the cooking.

GRAVY.

Remove the meat and rack from the pan, pour off nearly all the fat, dredge in flour, cook till brown; add hot water gradually, stir well, season with salt and pepper, simmer 5 m., strain.

FRANCONIA POTATOES.

Wash, scrub and pare potatoes of even size. Put on the rack with the meat and baste when you baste the meat.

YORKSHIRE PUDDING.

3 eggs. $\frac{1}{2}$ tsp. salt.
$\frac{3}{4}$ c. flour, (scant).   2 c. milk.

Beat the eggs hard for two minutes; add the salt

and the milk, pour a little into the middle of the flour, beat till perfectly smooth, then add the remainder. Grease the gem pans, have them piping hot, fill two-thirds full and bake thirty-five minutes in a hot oven. Baste with the roast beef gravy when you baste the meat.

BROILED STEAK.

Trim off all unnecessary fat, put into a well greased broiler with the fat edge of the steak farthest from the fire. As it broils the fat will run down and baste the meat. Turn every 10 seconds. Serve on hot platter.

BROILED HAMBURGH STEAK.

1 lb. meat from rump or round chopped very fine. Proceed as for broiled steak.

BEEF STEW WITH DUMPLINGS.

$\frac{1}{2}$ lb. beef,	$\frac{1}{4}$ c. carrot,
$\frac{1}{2}$ onion,	$\frac{1}{4}$ c. turnip,
$\frac{1}{2}$ ssp. salt,	2 potatoes,
$\frac{1}{2}$ tbsp. pepper,	Water to cover.

If you have any pieces from broiled, fried or roast beef, cut off the fat and use them; if not reserve half the meat. Put the bones and half the meat in a kettle, cover with cold water. Melt the fat, dredge the other half of the meat with salt, pepper and flour, and fry till brown in the fat. Brown the onions, put meat and onions in the kettle and cover with boiling water. Simmer till the meat is tender, 2 or 3 h. Half an hour before serving remove the fat and bones, add the turnips and carrots cut in

MEAT. 93

small dice, and the potatoes cut into quarters. When ready to serve, thicken with the flour mixed in a little cold water and stirred into the stew. Add seasoning and serve. If dumplings are made do not thicken it with the flour.

DUMPLINGS.

2 c. flour, 2 tsp. Cleveland's baking powder,
½ tsp. salt, 1 scant c. milk.

Sift the flour, salt and baking-powder together, add the milk, stirring very little. Drop at once by the spoonfuls into the boiling stew. Cover closely and cook 10 m. without removing the cover. Serve at once.

CORNED BEEF.

Always select a piece with some fat, and if very salt soak in cold water half an hour. Throw off this water and cover with fresh cold water; when it boils skim and simmer till tender. If the beef is allowed to cool in the water in which it is boiled it will not be as dry.

FILLET OF BEEF.

Remove all the muscle, ligament and thin, tough skin. If not in good shape skewer with small steel or wooden skewers. Lard with two rows of pork. Dredge with salt, pepper and flour. Put in a small baking-pan with small pieces of pork under. Put in a hot oven and bake 20 to 30 m. Do not bake even a large fillet over 30 m. Serve with mushroom, hollandaise or tomato sauce.

BEEF À LA MODE.

4 to 6 lbs. beef from the under part of the round.
3 tbsp. beef drippings, 2 tbsp. vinegar,
2 onions, 1 tbsp. lemon juice,
½ carrot, 1 tbsp. salt,
½ turnip, ½ tsp. pepper,
2 cloves, 1 sq. inch stick cinnamon,
6 allspice berries, 1 bay leaf,
1 sprig summer savory, 1 sprig thyme,
1 " sage, 1 " majoram,
4 tbsp. flour, 1 " parsley,
½ lb. fat salt pork.

Cut the pork in thick strips and put in a larding needle and draw through the meat; or you may make holes and push the pork into the meat. Cut the vegetables fine and cook till brown in the butter; remove the vegetables; dredge the meat with salt, pepper and flour, and brown on all sides in the fat in which the vegetables have been fried. Tie the herbs in a small piece of cheese cloth, add the water, herbs, spices, salt, pepper, vinegar and vegetables and simmer four hours, tightly covered. Take out the meat, skim off the fat and thicken the gravy with the flour mixed with a little cold water. This may be baked in the oven and should be kept closely covered, and basted occasionally.

FRIZZLED BEEF.

½ lb. smoked beef cut thin,
2 eggs, yolks and whites,
½ tbsp. butter.

Put the beef in a frying-pan, cover it with cold water, bring to a boil and boil five minutes. Drain off all the water, put the pan on the fire, add the butter, stir well when melted, add the well beaten eggs and stir till the eggs are firm. Serve at once.

MUTTON AND LAMB.

Next to beef, mutton is the most nutritious meat and is very easily digested. Some persons dislike the strong flavor, but a little care in preparing will remove a portion of it. The pink skin on the edge of the fat on chops should be removed, and the thin fat that is generally wrapped round a leg should not be used. Both of these increase the strong taste.

TO CHOOSE MUTTON.

Select a piece from a large, heavy animal, with plenty of hard, white fat, and the flesh bright red.

ROAST MUTTON.

The leg, loin, or fore-quarter may be used as a roast. Remove all the pink fat, skewer the loin by having the rib bones cracked, and fold over, or you can remove the bones and roll up, with stuffing inside or not. If the fore-quarter be used, remove the large bone, which is the shoulder blade, fill the cavity with stuffing and skewer into shape. This is a very economical and palatable roast. (See boned leg of lamb for stuffing.)

BOILED MUTTON.

Remove the fat, put into boiling water with 2 tbsp. salt. Boil 10 m., skim and simmer till the meat is tender. (See time-table for boiling, page 27.)

MUTTON AND LAMB.

GRAVY FOR MUTTON.

2 c. water in which the mutton was boiled, 2 tsp. flour, 2 tsp. vinegar, ½ ssp. pepper, 2 tbsp. chopped parsley, 1 ssp. salt. Mix the flour with a little cold water, stir into the boiling water, boil 5 m., stirring well; add parsley and seasoning.

MUTTON OR LAMB CHOPS. (Broiled.)

Wipe, remove the pink skin and extra fat. Put in a well greased broiler and broil over red, clear fire, turning every 10 seconds. Serve on hot dish.

CHOPS. (Pan Broiled.)

Wipe, remove the pink skin and extra fat. Heat a frying-pan very hot. Rub over once with a little fat, put in the chops, turn in 1 m., then turn every 2 m. till done. Will take 5 m. Stand on the fat edge to brown the fat. Drain on brown paper, sprinkle with salt and pepper and serve hot. Do not allow any fat to melt in the pan; drain off at once, or the chops will be fried instead of broiled.

BREADED LAMB CHOPS WITH STUFFED TOMATOES.

Select tender chops, 1 in. thick. Wipe, trim off all extra fat. Salt and pepper them. Cover with fine sifted bread crumbs. Lay on a rack in a baking-pan. For each chop take one ripe, round tomato. Cut a small circle off the opposite side to the stem. Scoop out a little of the tomato, fill the cavity with fine bread crumbs, seasoned with salt, pepper, sugar, a few drops of onion juice and a little melted butter. Cover with the circles cut off; stand one tomato on each chop and bake in a hot oven 20 to 30 m. Shield the tomatoes, if necessary, with greased paper. Decorate with sprigs of parsley. This is a very uncommon and delicious French dish.

CHOPS EN PAPILLOTE.

Use sheets of glazed white writing paper. Butter them on the inside with a pastry brush dipped in melted butter. Wipe and trim the chops, season with salt and pepper, and wrap in the buttered papers. Broil 5 or 6 m., taking care not to break or burn the paper, as this will let out the juice. Serve with tomato sauce, or you may prepare the following sauce: Cook 1 heaping tbsp. flour in 1 tbsp. butter, add slowly 1 c. boiling stock, $\frac{1}{2}$ tbsp. minced mushrooms, $\frac{1}{2}$ tbsp. minced parsley, a little lemon juice, $\frac{1}{2}$ ssp. salt, $\frac{1}{4}$ ssp. pepper. Broil the chops in the buttered papers 3 m. Remove from the papers and lay in clean papers, covering with the sauce; fold up and bake 10 m. in the oven.

CROWN OF LAMB.

Select a piece from the loin, containing only the rib bones. Have the butcher cut down between the ribs until you can turn the piece around in a circle, with the rib bones outside. Have the bones scraped of meat down to where the lean meat begins. Do not have the bones too long. Skewer into a circle, dredge with salt, pepper and flour, and bake in a hot oven, being careful not to burn the ends of the bones. You can protect them by laying greased paper over. Put a few pieces of fat under the rack and on top of the meat. Baste often. When done, trim the bones with a paper ruffle, and fill the circle in the centre with green peas, piling them up in a point, so that they may be seen above the meat. Make a gravy as for roast beef, or serve with currant jelly sauce.

BONED LEG OF LAMB OR MUTTON.

Remove the bone, salt it inside and put in the following stuffing: Mix 1 c. cracker crumbs with 1 ssp. salt, thyme, pepper, 1 tbsp. chopped onion, 1 tbsp. chopped parsley, ¼ c. melted butter. Sew up and dredge with salt, pepper, and flour. Put on a rack in a baking pan with small pieces of suet on the meat and in the pan. Cook in a hot oven about one hour for small leg, 1½ hours for large one. Serve with currant jelly sauce.

COTTAGE PIE.

Chop any cold meat very fine. To one cup of meat add 1 ssp. salt, ½ ssp. pepper, a few drops of onion juice, and ⅛ c. gravy or stock. Put meat, seasoning and gravy in a dish, cover with mashed potatoes and bake in the oven till brown.

SCALLOPED MUTTON.

Cut cold cooked mutton into thin pieces or cubes, removing all bone, fat and gristle. Season ½ c. fine bread crumbs with salt and pepper, put in bottom of a shallow baking dish, cover with meat, then boiled macaroni, and lastly add ¾ c. tomato sauce. Pour 1 tbsp. melted butter over ⅓ c. fine bread crumbs, and spread over the top. Bake about 20 m.

MINCED MEAT ON TOAST.

Remove all fat, gristle and bone. Chop very fine. Put in a saucepan ½ c. gravy, ¼ ssp. pepper, 1 ssp.

salt, a few drops of onion juice. Add 1 c. chopped meat, and when hot serve on toast.

SCOTCH BROTH.

½ c. barley. 2 tbsp. beef dripping.
2 lbs. neck mutton. 1 " flour.
2 qts. cold water. 2 tsp. salt.
1 ssp. white pepper. 1 ssp. chopped parsley.
¼ c. each carrot, turnip, onion, celery. ½c. tomato.

Soak the barley several hours. Wipe the meat, remove the fat. Cut the meat into small cubes and put on with the barley in 3 pts. of cold water. As it boils skim off the fat. Put on the bones in 1 pt. cold water. Cut the vegetables into ¼ inch dice, fry in half the drippings and add to the meat. Simmer until the meat is tender, about 3 h. Strain the water from the bones, cook the flour and the other half of the butter, add the strained water gradually, add the tomato, stir into the broth. Add salt, pepper and parsley. Simmer 10 m.

MUTTON RECHAUFFÉ.

1 lb. cold mutton. 1 egg.
1 tbsp. butter. 1 tbsp. chopped onion.
Yolk 1 egg. 2 " flour.

Slice the cold meat or cut into small pieces. Make a sauce as follows: Cook the onion in the butter till light yellow, add the dry flour, add ½ c. boiling water gradually, 1 ssp. salt, ¼ ssp. pepper and the yolk of one egg. Pour out on a dish. Oil the bottom of a shallow dish. Spread the slices of the cold meat with this sauce, laying side first spread on the dish. Roll in crumbs, egg and crumbs, and fry in hot cottolene.

VEAL.

Veal should be thoroughly cooked, as at best it is very indigestible. The flesh should be pink, never white, and the fat white. It is best in the spring, and should always be well seasoned, as it has less flavor than other meats.

ROAST VEAL.

May be prepared as roast mutton. Make the stuffing moist by adding a little water. Use pieces of lard to lay on top and under the meat, and after the first half hour, you may add a little water to the pan, to use in basting. The gravy made from the baking pan, if nice and brown, is the most delicious.

VEAL CUTLETS.

A slice of veal from the breast or the leg may be cut into pieces for serving, putting the small pieces together with a small wooden toothpick. Salt and pepper them and roll in fine bread crumbs. You may sauté them in a little fat or fry in deep, hot cottolene. Do not have the slices too thick, and cook till thoroughly done, allowing 5 m. for 1 inch thick.

VEAL CUTLET À LA PROVENÇALE.

1 tbsp. butter,
1 " chopped onion,
6 minced mushrooms,
$\frac{1}{4}$ tsp. mace,
1 bay leaf,
$1\frac{1}{4}$ c. stock,
1 c. tomato sauce No. 2,
Few drops lemon juice,
Salt and pepper to taste,
1 sprig thyme.

Fry the onion and mushrooms in the butter, add bay leaf, thyme, mace and stock; simmer 30 m. Press through a sieve, add tomato sauce, lemon, salt and pepper, simmer 5 minutes. Roll the cutlets in crumbs, egg and crumbs, and fry in hot fat 5 minutes. Pour the sauce over them and serve.

CASSEROLE OF MOCK SWEETBREADS.

1 lb. raw veal cut into $\frac{1}{2}$ inch cubes, cook in boiling salted water till tender with one slice of onion; drain, and put into cold water to whiten. Make 1 c. white sauce, add to it 1 ssp. celery salt and pepper if needed. Heat over hot water 5 m. Remove from the fire, and add quickly, 1 well beaten egg and 1 tsp. lemon juice. Serve in a border of rice or on toast.

PORK.

As pork is very unwholesome and indigestible, it should be very sparingly used, and never given to children or persons of weak digestion. It should never be used excepting in the winter, and then should be thoroughly cooked. The meat should be pale red, the fat white, the skin smooth and clear.

ROAST PIG.

The pig should be four or five weeks old. Clean, wash in cold water thoroughly, dry, stuff and sew up. Skewer the fore legs forward and the hind legs either forward or backward whichever you prefer; either way is used. Rub with butter, dredge with salt, pepper and flour, and put a little water in the pan and put in moderately hot oven, as it must be thoroughly done. Baste often with butter in a little hot water, and after, with the dripping in the pan. Roast two and a half or three hours. When done, serve decorated with parsley or celery, with a piece of either in the mouth, or a small red apple.

STUFFING.

1 c. bread crumbs, 1 tbsp. chopped parsley, 1 tsp. sage, 1 tsp. salt, ¼ tsp. black pepper, 1 tbsp. onion juice; mix all the ingredients together and moisten with 1 tbsp. butter in ¼ c. hot water.

ROAST PORK.

Wipe, and dredge with salt, pepper and flour. Cook in a moderate oven, allowing twenty-five minutes to every pound. Prepare the gravy the same as roast beef gravy and serve with apple sauce. Cold roast pork is very much better than hot.

PORK CHOPS.

Grease a hot frying-pan, salt and pepper the chops, lay in the pan and fry till brown. When done, pour off all the fat, shake a little flour in the pan, when brown add a little hot water, stirring well; cook 5 m., season with salt and pepper and pour over the chops.

PORK TENDERLOIN.

Prepare the same as pork chops

PORK AND BEANS.

1 qt. beans, ¼ lb. salt pork, 1 tsp. salt, ¼ c. molasses. Soak the beans over night in cold water. Throw off this water in the morning, put in cold water and simmer till tender, but not broken. Turn

them into a colander and pour cold water through. Put them into the bean pot or pan. Score the rind of the pork, bury it in the beans, leaving only the rind exposed. Put the salt into the molasses, add $\frac{1}{4}$ c. hot water and pour over the beans. Cover and bake in a moderate oven 6 h.

BOILED HAM.

Soak over night in cold water. Scrub with a small scrubbing brush, trim off the black part, cover with cold water, add a blade of mace, 3 cloves and a bay leaf, and simmer till tender, about a half hour to a pound. Let it remain in the water till cold, peel off the rind, sprinkle with bread crumbs, and brown in the oven; or decorate with cloves and parsley. Trim the shank bone with a paper frill.

HAM AND EGGS.

Have the ham in slices half an inch thick; remove the rind, gash the fat and cut into small pieces for serving. Put into a hot frying-pan with no fat, fry over a quick fire till the fat is crisp. Break as many eggs as you have pieces of ham, taking care not to break the yolk, and drop one at a time in the hot fat left from cooking the ham. You may put muffin rings into the pan and drop an egg into each; this will keep the eggs round. Cook slowly until the yolks are set, lift up carefully and put one egg on each piece of ham.

CREAMED HAM.

1 pt. lean cold boiled ham cut into $\frac{1}{2}$ inch dice, 1 c. white sauce, spk. cayenne, $\frac{1}{4}$ tsp. mustard. Cut up the ham, make the sauce, leaving out the salt

until you add the ham, for fear it might be too salt, add the cayenne, mustard and ham. Serve in dresden patty cases, or in potato border, or on toast.

LIVER AND BACON.

Cut the bacon in thin slices and the liver into serving pieces. Scald the liver, dredge with salt, pepper and flour. Put the bacon in a frying-pan with no fat, fry till crisp, lay on a hot dish; then put the liver into the hot fat, fry on one side, turn over and brown on the other side. Put on the dish with a piece of bacon on each piece of liver.

TO TRY OUT LARD.

Cut the leaves in small pieces, put on the back of the stove and cook slowly till crisp; strain through a fine sieve or cloth into pails.

POULTRY AND GAME.

TO CHOOSE GOOD POULTRY.

Turkeys should have the lower end of the breast bone soft, full, plump breasts, the flesh firm and white.

Chickens should have firm flesh, plump breast, soft yellow feet, smooth legs, and the cartilage at the end of the breast bone should be soft and pliable.

Geese and ducks have the same tests as chickens, the breast being hard and thick, the windpipe breaking under pressure of the thumb and finger.

TO TRUSS AND DRESS POULTRY.

Pick out all the pin-feathers, singe over a little burning paper, holding in the flame and taking care not to touch the burnt paper, or it will blacken it; wipe all over with a damp cloth. Cut off the head, push back the skin off the neck and close to the body; take hold of the windpipe and work down carefully to the crop, remove and cut off close to the body. Make an incision three inches long near the tail, lengthwise of the fowl; insert two fingers and work up carefully, keeping close to the breast bone until you reach the liver and heart, push the fingers around on both sides; when all seems to be loose, grasp the entire entrails, having the fingers above the liver and the heart and around the gizzard, and pull out carefully. Be very careful not to break the gall bladder, which is a small, green bag, that lies under the liver. Remove the kidneys and the lungs, which lie in the back between the ribs. Remove the oil bag in the tail. Wipe inside and out, but never put in water unless you have broken some of the entrails, and then wash very quickly and dry at once. Salt the inside, stuff and skewer or sew up, run a skewer through the tail, tie the legs together, push them well up into the body; hold in place with a skewer run through the upper part of the leg and through the body; tie the ends of the legs to the skewer through the tail. Turn the tips of the wings back, skewer close to the body, fill the skin where the crop was with stuffing, tie up the neck and fasten the end under the back.

TO CLEAN THE GIBLETS.

Remove the liver, cut off all discolored parts, cut the veins out of the heart, cut through the gizzard, remove the inside lining, use only the meat part, cutting close to the gristle, wash and put in cold water till tender.

boil

ROAST CHICKEN.

Clean, stuff and truss; lay on a rack in a baking pan, rub with soft butter, dredge with salt and flour. Lay any chicken fat over the top of the chicken and in the pan. If you have not enough, use beef drippings. Baste often. Use no water at first, but later on add a little at a time. Turn the chicken so that it may brown on all sides. Bake until the joints begin to separate. About 1½ h. for a 4 lb. chicken. When done draw out the threads and skewers, lay on a platter and garnish with celery or parsley.

STUFFING.

1 c. bread crumbs, 1 tbsp. melted butter, ½ tsp. sage, ½ tsp. thyme, ½ tsp. salt, ⅓ tsp. pepper. You can use a little onion juice, chopped celery, or oysters, if you like.

GIBLET GRAVY.

Pour off all the grease from the baking pan, dredge with a little flour; when brown add a little hot water gradually, salt and pepper; cook 5 m., strain, and add the giblets which have been chopped fine.

ROAST TURKEY.

Prepare the same as roast chicken. You may lay two or three sausages on top of the turkey while roasting; they baste it and give a delicious flavor.

BOILED CHICKEN.

The chicken should be over a year old and not too fat. Clean, stuff and truss as for roasting. Dredge with salt and flour, and put in a pot with just enough water to cover. Add one bay leaf and a quarter of a cup of washed rice. Cover closely and simmer till tender; allow 30 m. to a lb. When done, lay on a hot platter and serve with brown sauce, adding ½ c. chopped celery or a few capers.

BROILED CHICKEN.

Only a very tender, young chicken is suitable for broiling. Singe, split down the back; break the joints, remove the breast bone, clean and wipe out. Rub with soft butter and sprinkle with salt and pepper. Put in a well greased broiler and broil 20

m. Turn the inside to the fire first. When done, serve on hot dish, seasoned with salt, pepper and butter. Can be served also with tartar sauce, or maitre d'hotel butter.

CHICKEN FRICASSEE.

Clean, cut at the joints for serving, cover with boi ing water, add 2 tsp. salt, 1 ssp. pepper and 1 bay leaf. Simmer till tender. Remove the large bones and return to the water; dredge the meat with a very little salt and pepper, roll in fine bread crumbs and fry in hot drippings or deep fat. Drain on paper and serve on toast.

GRAVY.

1 tbsp. butter, 1 c. milk, 1 tsp. lemon juice, 2 tbsp. flour, $\frac{1}{4}$ tsp. celery salt, 1 c. chicken broth, 1 ssp. white pepper. Heat the milk, cook the flour and butter together till smooth, add the milk gradually, beating well; add the broth and seasoning.

CASSEROLE OF RICE AND CHICKEN.

$1\frac{1}{2}$ c. cooked meat, 1 c. cooked rice, 2 tbsp. bread crumbs, $\frac{3}{4}$ tsp. salt, 1 ssp. pepper, 1 ssp. thyme, 1 ssp. majoram, $\frac{1}{2}$ tsp. chopped onion, 1 tsp. chopped parsley, 1 ssp. celery salt, 1 egg, 1 tsp. lemon juice, about 1 scant c. of stock. Chop the meat fine, add the stock and seasoning. Butter a 3 pt. mold, cover with the crumbs, then rice on sides and bottom $\frac{1}{2}$ in. thick; fill the cavity with the meat, cover with rice, cover the mold and bake $\frac{1}{2}$ h. or steam $\frac{3}{4}$ of an hour. Serve with tomato sauce No. 1.

CHICKEN SAUTÉ.

Remove the bones from cold boiled chicken, dredge with a little salt and pepper, and roll in crumbs, egg and crumbs, and fry in hot cottolene. Lay on toast in a border of hot white sauce, with small flowerettes of hot boiled cauliflower.

CREAMED CHICKEN.

Cut cold cooked chicken into small pieces; to 1 c. meat allow 1 c. white sauce. Make the sauce, add ¼ tsp. celery salt, 2 drops onion juice, add the chicken, salt and pepper if needed; warm through, remove from the fire, add ½ tsp. lemon juice, and serve on toast, in potato border, or in dresden patty cases. Any bits of cold meat may be used up in this way.

CHICKEN WITH MUSHROOMS.

The white meat of a cold roast or boiled chicken cut into cubes, can of mushrooms, ¾ c. milk, ¾ c. chicken broth, 1 egg, ¼ c. butter, 2 tsp. cornstarch, ⅓ c. chopped celery, salt and pepper to taste. Cook the butter and cornstarch till smooth, add the hot broth gradually, then the hot milk, then the well-beaten egg. Cook 1 m., stirring, add chicken, mushroom, celery; season with salt and pepper; serve on toast or in patty cases.

CHICKEN HOLLANDAISE.

½ c. butter, yolks of two eggs, juice ½ lemon, ¼ ssp. cayenne, 1 tsp. chopped parsley, 1 ssp. chopped onion, 1 tsp. cornstarch, 2 c. hot chicken broth, 2 c. chicken chopped fine, ¾ c. celery chopped fine. Cook the onion in the butter 1 m., add the cornstarch, cook till smooth, add the broth gradually, then add the beaten yolks, then the celery; season with salt and pepper, add the chicken. Serve with graham toast.

ROAST DUCK.

Prepare the same as for roast chicken. You may stuff them or not as you please. The strong odor can be removed partly, by stuffing with quartered apples, cored and pared. Do not use the apples. Serve with apple sauce or cranberries. Bake 30 m. in a hot oven.

ROAST GOOSE.

Before drawing wash and scrub thoroughly in warm soapsuds. Rinse off. Draw, wash out the inside and proceed as for roast chicken, laying slices of fat salt pork over the breast. This will baste the meat, so do not rub with soft butter. When half done, pour off the grease from the pan, remove the pork and dredge with flour. Add a little water to the pan and baste when the flour browns. Cook until brown and tender, allowing twenty-five minutes to a pound. Serve with giblet sauce, as for roast chicken, and apple sauce.

LARDED GROUSE.

Clean, wipe inside and out. Turn the wings back, fasten the legs to the sides of the body; put two rows of lardoons down the breast and one row on the legs. Run small skewer through the tail. Tie the legs firmly to this skewer. Dredge with salt; rub the breast with soft butter, then dredge with flour. Cook 20 m. in a hot oven. Baste every 5 m.

Remove from the pan, lay on the bread sauce and cover with browned crumbs.

BREAD SAUCE.

1 pt. milk, 1 quarter onion, 1 c. soft bread crumbs. Put the milk and onion in a double boiler with $\frac{1}{3}$ of a cup of fine bread crumbs; cook 15 m., add 1 tsp. salt, 1 ssp. pepper. Brown the $\frac{2}{3}$ c. coarse bread crumbs in 1 tbsp. butter; lay over the grouse.

QUAIL.

Quail may be larded like grouse, and baked and served on toast, with cubes of currant jelly; or it may be boned and wrapped in buttered paper and broiled; or the breasts may be cooked in a sweet potato, hollowing out the potato by cutting through the middle; put the breast in, tie up and cook till the potato is done. Tie up with a ribbon and decorate with a sprig of parsley. The bones should always be stewed down to make stock for rich sauces.

MEAT AND FISH SAUCES.

WHITE SAUCE.

1 c. milk, 1 tbsp. flour, 1 tbsp. butter, ¼ tsp. salt, ¼ ssp. white pepper. Heat the milk, mix the flour, salt and pepper, cook the butter 1 m., add the dry flour, cook till smooth, add the milk gradually, stirring hard all the time; when half the milk is added, remove from the fire and give a thorough beating; add the rest of the milk slowly; cook 2 m. after all is used. It will curdle and lump when you first begin to add the milk, but stir well and it will come out smooth. Take care that the butter or flour does not brown.

CREAM SAUCE.

Prepare the same as white sauce, using cream instead of milk.

BROWN SAUCE.

1 pt. stock, 2 tbsp. flour, 2 tbsp. butter, ½ tsp. salt, 1 ssp. pepper, 2 tbsp. chopped onion, ½ tbsp. lemon juice, 1 tbsp. carrot. Cook the vegetables in the butter till the onion is light brown, add the dry flour; when brown add the hot stock slowly, stir well all the time; when half the stock is used give a thorough beating; add the remaining stock, salt and pepper. Cook 5 m. and strain. The stock for sauces may be made by putting chop, steak, game, or any small bits of bone or meat in cold water, and boiling slowly for 6 hours.

BROWN MUSHROOM SAUCE, FOR FILLETS, VEAL CUTLETS, ETC.

Add to the brown sauce ½ c. of the liquor from a can of mushrooms, and ½ can of mushrooms cut in quarters.

BROWN SAUCE PIQUANT.

To 1 c. brown sauce add 1 tbsp. each of chopped pickles, onions, and parsley.

CURRANT JELLY SAUCE. (For mutton.)

To 1 c. brown sauce add ½ c. currant jelly; boil up once and serve.

DRAWN BUTTER.

1 pt. hot stock, or water, ⅓ c. butter, 2 tbsp. flour, ½ tsp. salt, ½ ssp. pepper. Prepare as for white sauce.

CAPER SAUCE.

Add to the drawn butter sauce 4 tbsp. capers and 1 tbsp. vinegar.

PARSLEY SAUCE.

Add to the drawn butter sauce 2 tbsp. chopped parsley.

EGG SAUCE.

Add two or three hard boiled eggs, chopped.

SHRIMP SAUCE.

Add 1 c. shrimps, whole, or chopped fine, 1 tbsp. lemon juice and a few grains of cayenne.

OYSTER SAUCE.

Cook 1 pt. oysters till plump; drain and use 1 pt.

MEAT AND FISH SAUCES. 115

of the liquor for drawn butter sauce. Add 1 ssp. celery salt and a speck of cayenne. Add the oysters and cook 1 m.

LOBSTER SAUCE.

Reserve ½ c. of tender bits of meat. Cut remainder fine, simmer in 1 pt. hot water 1 h. Pound the coral with 1 tbsp. butter to a paste. Cook 1½ tbsp. flour in 2 tbsp. butter till smooth, strain and add the water, ¼ ssp. cayenne, ½ tbsp. lemon juice, the lobster, butter, and bits of meat.

TOMATO SAUCE. No. 1.

1 tbsp. butter, 1 tbsp. flour, 1 tbsp. chopped onion, 1 c. mutton liquor or stock, ½ c. strained tomato, 1 tsp. salt, 1 ssp. pepper. Heat the stock, fry the onion in the butter till light yellow, add the flour and the salt and pepper, when smooth and frothy add the stock gradually; add the tomato.

TOMATO SAUCE. No. 2.

1 pt. tomato.	½ ssp. pepper.
½ " hot water.	1 tsp. salt.
1 tbsp. chopped onion.	2 allspice berries.
1 " butter.	2 whole cloves.
1 " flour.	2 peppercorns.
1 sprig thyme.	2 sprigs of parsley.
1 " parsley.	1 sprig majoram.
1 " summer savory.	1 " sage.
1 bay leaf.	

Cook the tomato, water, spices, herbs, parsley 10 m. Cook the onion in the butter till yellow, add the dry flour, when smooth and frothy add the tomato. Boil 10 m. and strain.

HOLLANDAISE SAUCE.

½ c. butter, yolks 3 eggs, 1 tbsp. lemon juice, 1 ssp. salt, ¼ ssp. pepper (cayenne), ⅓ c. boiling water. Cream the butter; add the yolks, one at a time, beat well; add the seasoning. Add the boiling water, set the bowl in a pan of boiling water and stir till it thickens. When thick as cream, remove at once, or it will curdle.

BÉCHAMEL SAUCE.

1 tbsp. butter.	1½ c. white stock.
1 " flour.	1 spk. nutmeg.
½ c. cream.	Yolks of 2 eggs.
1 tbsp. lemon juice.	

(5 peppercorns, 1 blade of mace, 1 bay leaf, ½ slice onion, 1 sprig parsley and thyme, 1 slice carrot, tied in a cloth.)

Cook the little bag in the stock ½ hour; heat the cream, cook the flour and butter till frothy, add the stock, removing the bag, add the cream, pour on to the beaten egg, return to the fire and cook over hot water till it thickens like custard, being careful not to curdle; remove from the fire, add the lemon juice and nutmeg, salt and pepper, if needed.

TARTAR SAUCE. (Hot, for fish.)

1 tbsp. vinegar, 1 tsp. lemon juice, 1 ssp. salt, 1 tbsp. Worcestershire sauce, ¼ c. butter. Mix vinegar, lemon juice, salt and sauce in bowl, over hot water, brown the butter in a small pan and add to the other.

MAYONNAISE TARTAR.

½ c. oil.
3 tbsp. vinegar.
¼ tsp. onion juice.
Yolks 2 raw eggs.

1 tsp. salt.
¼ " pepper.
1 " mustard.
1 " sugar.

1 tbsp. each chopped olives, capers, pickles, and parsley. Make the same as Mayonnaise, adding the chopped ingredients last.

MAITRE D'HOTEL BUTTER.

¼ c. butter.
½ tsp. salt.
½ ssp. white pepper.

1 tbsp. lemon juice.
1 " chopped parsley.

Cream the butter, add the seasoning and stir well. Serve on steak, Hamburgh steak, or fish.

ROMOULADE SAUCE.

2 tbsp. vinegar.
2 " tarragon vinegar.
1 ssp. cayenne.
Yolk 1 raw egg.

1 tsp. mustard.
½ " salt.
1 " chopped parsley.
¾ c. olive oil.

Yolks of 2 hard boiled eggs.

Mash the yolks, add the raw yolk, seasoning, beat well; add the oil very slowly, beating well; when too thick add a little vinegar. Add the vinegar slowly and parsley last.

SWEETBREADS.

TO PREPARE SWEETBREADS.

The best sweetbreads come from veal and are large glands, one lying in the back of the throat, the other in the breast, near the heart. The heart sweetbread is the best. They spoil very quickly and should be immediately placed in cold water with a little salt as soon as they come from the market. Let them stand 1 h., as this draws out all the blood, then remove all the pipes and membranes, and put into boiling salted water with 1 tbsp. lemon juice. Boil 15 m. and plunge into cold water to harden and whiten. They may then be put away for future use, but should be kept in a very cold place and used within twenty-four hours. Do not cook in either iron or tin, and always cut with a silver knife.

CREAMED SWEETBREADS.

Cut prepared sweetbreads into small cubes. For $\frac{1}{2}$ c. sweetbreads make 1 c. white sauce, add the sweetbreads, $\frac{1}{2}$ c. mushrooms quartered, heat for a few moments over hot water, serve on toast with green peas around, or in cases. You may leave out the mushrooms and add more sweetbreads.

SWEETBREADS IN CASES.

Break or cut prepared sweetbreads into small sections or cubes. Scald 1 c. cream in the double boiler. Beat the yolks of 2 eggs, pour the cream over, return to the fire and cook till thick as custard, stirring all the time. Remove from the fire, add the sweetbreads, season with salt and pepper, fill the cases, cover with buttered crumbs, and bake till the crumbs are brown.

BROILED SWEETBREADS.

Rub prepared sweetbreads with butter, salt and pepper, wrap in buttered paper and broil 10 m. Serve on toast with Maître d'Hôtel butter.

SWEETBREADS AND BACON.

Cut prepared sweetbreads into $\frac{1}{2}$ inch cubes, roll in crumbs, egg and crumbs. Put one cube on a wooden toothpick, then a small thin square slice of bacon, etc., using three pieces of each on one skewer. Fry in hot cottolene and serve on the skewers with tomato sauce No. 2.

LARDED SWEETBREADS.

Trim prepared sweetbreads, remove all fat and put five lardoons in each; dredge with salt, pepper and flour, lay on a rack in a baking pan, bake in a hot oven 30 m., basting with brown stock. Drain the liquor from a can of very small French peas, rinse them in cold water, drain, and put on the fire in fresh cold water; let it come to a boil, drain the peas again, add a little butter, pepper, salt and very little sugar. When hot pile on a platter, cover with white sauce and put the sweetbreads on top. Garnish with parsley. The two cold waters used on the peas helps to remove the taste of the can. This is a very delicious and attractive dish for an entrée.

For sweetbread croquettes and salad, look for croquettes and salads.

VEGETABLES.

POTATOES.

Potatoes consist of three-fourths water, nearly one-fourth starch, with a small amount of mineral matter; potash salts and silica. They are easily digested, particularly when baked in a hot oven. They should always be served as soon as cooked, as standing makes them less palatable.

BOILED POTATOES.

Select ones of the same size and shape; wash, scrub, pare and put in cold water. Put in boiling salted water, allowing 1 tsp. salt to 1 quart of water. Boil gently till they can be pierced with a fork, drain at once every drop of water off, shake gently so as to break the outside a little, and let the dry starch inside give them a mealy appearance. Set on the side of the stove uncovered for a few minutes.

BAKED POTATOES.

Wash and scrub potatoes of medium size and bake in a hot oven from 30 to 45 m., or until soft. As soon as they are done break the skins so that they may let out the steam and be mealy. Serve at once uncovered.

MASHED POTATOES.

While you are boiling the potatoes get everything ready; a hot dish, potato masher, a fork, pepper, salt, butter, and a little hot milk. As soon as the potatoes are drained, mash at once in the same

VEGETABLES. 121

saucepan ; do not mash by patting them down but with a quick, sharp motion bring the masher down to the bottom of the pan each time. Scrape around the corners with a fork and mash again. When all the lumps are out (and the quicker it is done the more delicious will be the potatoes) add a little pepper, salt, butter and hot milk and beat very light.

POTATO CAKES.

Make cold mashed potato into small, round cakes $\frac{1}{2}$ in. thick. Put a little butter in a frying-pan, just enough to grease it all over, put in the cakes and cook till brown. Turn with a knife, brown the other side and serve on hot dish.

POTATO BALLS.

Season 1 pt. hot mashed potato with pepper, salt, celery salt, chopped parsley and butter ; beat 1 egg very light ; add half to the potato. Shape into round balls, roll in remainder of egg, bake on buttered tin till brown. Serve round Hamburgh steak.

RICE POTATO.

Press hot mashed potato through a colander into a hot dish, and put in the oven till brown. Serve uncovered.

CREAMED POTATOES.

1 pt. cold boiled potatoes, $\frac{1}{2}$ c. milk, spk. white pepper, 1 tbsp. butter, $\frac{1}{2}$ tsp. salt, 1 tsp. parsley. Cut the potatoes into small dice. Put the milk in a frying-pan, add the seasoning, when hot add the potatoes ; when the milk is nearly absorbed, add the butter, stir gently with a fork so as not to break

them. Cook 5 m., turn into a dish, sprinkle the parsley over them and serve.

LYONNAISE POTATOES.

1 pt. cold boiled potatoes, ½ tsp. salt, ½ ssp. pepper, tbsp. chopped onion, 1 tbsp. beef dripping, 1 tbsp. chopped parsley. Cut the potatoes in small cubes; heat the dripping, fry the onion in it till light brown, add the potato, cook until brown, add the seasoning and chopped parsley.

FRANCONIA POTATOES.

Scrub and pare potatoes of uniform size, lay on the rack around the roast beef, bake with the meat and serve around the meat. When you baste the meat, pour the fat over the potatoes too.

FRIED POTATOES NO. 1.

Scrub, pare and cut in the desired shape, lay in cold salted water 1 h. Drain from the water, dry on a towel, and fry in hot cottolene.

FRIED OR SAUTÉD POTATOES, NO. 2

Cut cold boiled potatoes into slices ½ inch thick. Put some beef drippings in a frying-pan, when smoking hot put in enough potatoes to cover the pan; when brown turn on the other side and brown, lay on a hot dish, sprinkle with salt and pepper.

POTATO BALLS IN CREAM.

Scrub and pare good sized potatoes. With a vegetable cutter scoop out balls and lay them in cold water. Cook in boiling salted water until the balls are soft through, but not at all broken. While they are cooking make enough white sauce to cover them with ; when done, drain, and turn carefully into the white sauce. Sprinkle a little chopped parsley over and serve.

POTATOES A LA MAITRE D' HOTEL.

Scrub, pare, and cut into balls. Boil in salted water 10 m. Drain, barely cover with milk; when nearly absorbed add the butter.

MAITRE D'HOTEL BUTTER.

Cream 1 tbsp. butter, add the yolk of 1 raw egg, stir well, add 1 tsp. lemon juice, 1 tbsp. parsley, $\frac{1}{2}$ tsp. salt, $\frac{1}{2}$ ssp. pepper.

BOILED SWEET POTATOES.

Scrub, but do not pare. Cook in boiling salted water till tender. Peel at once, scraping off any of the dark part under the skin.

FRIED SWEET POTATOES.

Prepare the same as fried potatoes No. 2.

ESCALOPED SWEET POTATOES.

Cut cold boiled potatoes into $\frac{1}{2}$ inch cubes. Put a layer of potatoes on a platter, cover with white sauce, then another layer of potatoes and sauce. Cover with soft, white bread crumbs, not too small, and over which has been poured a little melted butter. Bake till the crumbs are brown.

BOILED TURNIPS.

Wash, cut into pieces, pare, and lay in cold water, cook in boiling salted water till tender; drain thoroughly, mash till free from lumps, add a little butter, pepper, and salt.

SCALLOPED TURNIPS.

Wash, pare, and cut into ½ in. cubes; cook in boiling salted water till tender. Drain, put a layer of turnips in a dish, cover with white sauce, then another layer of turnip; cover with sauce and cover the top with large, buttered bread crumbs. Bake till brown.

GREEN VEGETABLES.

Green vegetables should be kept in a cool place until used, and are improved by standing in cold water an hour before cooking. They should be cooked rapidly in boiling salted water, uncovered, and served as soon as done.

SPINACH.

Pick over and cut off the roots, wash thoroughly from one pan to another, and put in a kettle with no water, and a little salt; cook slowly at first, boil until tender. Drain, chop fine, season with salt, pepper, and butter. Garnish with hard boiled egg.

SPINACH A LA CREME.

After the spinach has been cooked and seasoned, mix with it a little white sauce, pile up in a mound and cover with white sauce; decorate with hard boiled egg.

PEAS.

Shell, lay in cold water if at all wilted, cook in boiling salted water until tender. Use only a little water, and let it boil away, so there is only a little left when the peas are done. Two or three pods cooked with the peas for ten minutes makes them sweeter. Add a little butter, pepper, and if they are not sweet, a little bit of sugar.

STRING BEANS.

Remove the strings from both sides of the beans, cut into inch pieces, cook in boiling salted water, the same as peas.

BEETS.

Cut the tops off about 2 inches from the beet; if you cut the beet at all it will bleed in cooking and lose its sweetness. Wash, and cook in boiling salted water with the skin on, until they are tender right through when pierced with a fork. When done, remove from the hot water and rub off the skins by holding in cold water. Cut in quarters, or slices, put a little butter on and serve.

ASPARAGUS.

Cut off the tough, white ends. Lay in cold water 1 h. before cooking. Tie securely into bundles, cook in boiling, salted water about 15 m., or till tender. While the asparagus is cooking, make enough toast to cover the platter it is served on, butter the toast, cover the toast with white sauce; lift out each bundle carefully by the cord, lay on the toast, the heads all one way, cut the cords with a scissors and cover the tips with a little sauce.

BOILED CABBAGE.

Remove all the leaves by breaking off one at a time close to the stalk, and lay them in large pan of cold water one hour. Have a large saucepan of boiling water, add 1 tsp. of salt, dry each leaf on a towel and drop into the water. Do not put in so many that the water will stop boiling; cook uncovered till tender, about twenty minutes. Drain in a colander and cut up lightly with a knife and fork. Put into a hot dish, season with salt, pepper, and butter, and serve. Some think it is improved by cooking in two waters.

CABBAGE A LA CREME.

Prepare as for boiled cabbage. Mix a little white sauce through it and cover with white sauce.

BOILED CAULIFLOWER.

Pick off the outside leaves and cut off any dark spots; cut off the stem close to the bottom of the flowerets. Soak in cold, salted water, top downwards, for one hour. Tie in a piece of cheese cloth to prevent breaking, and cook in boiling, salted water about fifteen or twenty minutes, or until a fork will pierce the stalk easily. When done, drain carefully, and serve, covered with white sauce.

CAULIFLOWER AU GRATIN.

Cook the cauliflower in boiling, salted water, till tender, or you may use any left over pieces. Break in small pieces, cover with white sauce, and soft, buttered bread crumbs, and bake till the crumbs are brown.

BORDER OF CAULIFLOWER.

Prepare as for boiled cauliflower, breaking the cauliflower into small flowerets. When the cauliflower is done, drain, and arrange around the dish as a border, pour white sauce over it and around it.

BOILED SPINACH.

Cut off the roots, pick off all the decayed and yellow leaves, and lay in cold water, Wash thoroughly from one panful of water to another, until the water is clear, and the sand all removed. Rinse and put into a pot with *no water*. Heat slowly and cook uncovered, adding a little salt. When tender, drain, chop fine and season with salt, pepper, and butter. Spinach is best cooked in its own juices, as it retains more of the mineral matter, its most valuable constituent.

ONIONS.

Lay in cold water and remove the skins. Cook in boiling, salted water until easily pierced with a fork; drain, add a little salt, pepper, butter, and hot milk

CORN ON THE COB.

Keep in cool place till ready to cook; remove the husks and every thread of silk. Put into boiling water with *no salt*, and after it comes to a boil cook five minutes. Pick up with a fork and lay on a napkin. Salt in the water is apt to turn the corn yellow.

LIMA BEANS.

Shell just before using, and cook in boiling, salted water, till the largest ones are soft. Drain, cook $\frac{1}{2}$ tbsp. butter and $\frac{1}{2}$ tsp. flour together, add 1 c. hot milk gradually, add the beans and season with salt and pepper.

SUCCOTASH.

1 pt. lima beans, 1 pt. of corn, $\frac{1}{2}$ pt. milk, $\frac{3}{4}$ tbsp. butter, $\frac{1}{2}$ ssp. pepper, salt, if needed. Cook the beans in boiling salted water till tender; run a sharp knife down through the centre of the kernels of the corn, cut or scrape the corn from the cob, being careful not to cut into the cob; put in a sauce-pan with the beans and milk, cook 5 m., add the butter, pepper, salt, if needed, and $\frac{1}{2}$ tsp sugar; boil up once and serve.

TOMATOES. (Raw.)

Pour boiling water over them, let stand 3 m., take

out and remove the skins. When cold put on the
ice, and when ready to serve cut in slices.

STEWED TOMATOES.

Scald, remove the skin and hard green stem. Cut
in small pieces and stew, uncovered, for 15 m., chopping with a spoon as they cook. Season with salt,
pepper, and a little sugar.

SCALLOPED TOMATOES.

Scald, remove the skins and cut in slices one half
inch thick. Butter a dish and put in a layer of fine
seasoned bread crumbs, then a layer of tomato;
season with a little salt, pepper, and sugar, then
another layer of crumbs. Two layers of crumbs and
two of tomato are enough, and cover the top with
$\frac{3}{4}$ c. crumbs, on which has been poured $\frac{1}{4}$ c. melted
butter. Bake until brown.

STUFFED TOMATOES.

Cut a small round from the opposite side to the
stem. Scoop out a little of the inside; fill the cavity
with fine bread crumbs, well seasoned with salt, pepper, and shake a very little sugar into the tomato
before putting in the stuffing. Cover with the small
rounds and bake in a hot oven about 20 m.

BRUSSELS SPROUTS IN CREAM.

1 qt. sprouts, 1 c. milk, 2 tbsp. butter, 1 tbsp.
flour, $\frac{1}{2}$ tsp. salt, $\frac{1}{8}$ tsp. pepper. Pick over and lay
the sprouts in cold water for 1 h. Drain and cook
in boiling salted water 30. m. Drain and put into
a double boiler with the milk; cook 10 m. Cream
the butter, add the flour, add a little hot milk; pour

onto the sprouts, cook five minutes, add the salt and pepper.

VEGETABLES A LA JARDINIERE.

1 can French peas. 1 pt. carrot ½ in. cubes.
3 gills stock (white). 1 " turnip "   "
3 tbsp. butter. 3 tsp. sugar.
3 tsp. salt.

Cook the vegetables in separate saucepans. When tender, drain, add to each ⅓ of the butter, salt, sugar and stock. Boil rapidly till the stock is absorbed. Spread the turnips on a platter, heap the carrots on the turnips, leaving a border of an inch; flatten the carrots and heap the peas on them. To prepare the canned peas, look for directions on canned vegetables, and then add the stock, etc., as directed.

FRIED EGG PLANT.

Cut in half-inch slices, pare, and put in strong, salted water to draw out the bitter taste. Allow two tablespoonfuls of salt to one quart of water. Keep under the water by laying saucers over it. Soak for two or three hours. Dry between towels, dip in crumbs, egg and crumbs, and fry in a little hot cottolene.

MUSHROOMS.

Mushrooms have a peculiarly delicious flavor, and are used for sauces and entreés. When purchased fresh, they should be bought of a reliable dealer, and unless you are able to distinguish the poisonous ones it is best to use the canned ones. One test is to stir, while boiling, with a silver spoon, and it will discolor if there is one poisonous one in the number. The skin should peel off easily from good mushrooms.

STEWED MUSHROOMS.

Peel the mushrooms, break into pieces or not as you choose, wash them, put in a granite pan, sprinkle slightly with a little salt and pepper, add to every pint of mushrooms one tablespoonful of butter rubbed into one tablespoonful of flour. Stew until tender, add a little cream, when hot, serve on toast.

BAKED MUSHROOMS.

Peel and cut off the stalks close to the top. Put on a baking dish upside down, sprinkle with salt and pepper and a little melted butter. Bake in a quick oven 20 m., basting with butter often. Serve as a garnish to meat.

BOILED MACARONI.

Cook in boiling salted water till tender, about 20 minutes. Drain in a colander and pour cold water through it. Serve with tomato sauce.

MACARONI AND CHEESE.

Prepare as for boiled macaroni ; put a layer in a deep baking dish, cover with a layer of cheese and a few little pieces of butter, then another layer of macaroni and cheese, covering the top of the dish with a thick layer of cheese. Add enough milk to come half way up the dish, and cook in a hot oven till the milk is almost absorbed.

SPAGHETTI.

$\frac{1}{4}$ lb. spaghetti. 2 tbsp. butter,
1 c. bread crumbs, 1 pt. tomato sauce No. 2.
1 c. grated cheese.

Cook the spaghetti in boiling salted water 20 m. Drain and pour cold water over it. Butter a platter, put on a layer of sauce, then one of spaghetti, sprinkle well with cheese; continue till all the material is used. Stir the crumbs into the melted butter, spread over the top and bake $\frac{1}{2}$ hour.

GRAINS.

Wheat, oats, corn, rye, barley, rice and buckwheat are the grains containing the most nutriment. The whole wheat grain contains all the elements for perfect food. Oatmeal is the most nutritious, containing more nitrogen than any other grain, and supplies material for hard work, both of brain and muscle. Corn contains more fat than other grains and so produces more heat. Rye is very nutritive, contains a good deal of sugar, and produces a good deal of heat. Barley is rich in phosphates, easily digested, contains starch and mucilage which make it valuable for the sick room. Rice is very easily digested, contains more starch and less fat than any other grain. Buckwheat contains more heat producing food than any other grain and is inferior in nutritive qualities. It should only be used in winter, and by those who exercise freely.

OATMEAL.

1 qt. boiling water.   1 c. oatmeal.   1 tsp. salt.

Put all into the top of a double boiler, place the boiler on the fire, let it boil rapidly for 10 m., stirring occasionally with a fork, place over the hot water and steam 1 to 2 h., according to the coarseness of the oatmeal.

HOMINY.

Prepare the same as oatmeal.

CRACKED WHEAT.

1 c. cracked wheat.   3 c. boiling water.   1 tsp. salt.
Cook the same as oatmeal, boiling it four hours.

STEAMED RICE.

½ c. rice.   ½ tsp. salt.   1 c. boiling water.

Wash the rice thoroughly, put it with the salt and water into the top of the double boiler, boil rapidly 10 m. stirring with a fork, then place over hot water and steam 20 m. Do not stir after you put it over the hot water, and keep it closely covered.

BOILED RICE.

1 c. rice.   3 qts. boiling water.   1 tsp. salt.

Wash the rice, put in the boiling water and boil rapidly until the kernels are soft. The time varies, about 30 m. Drain in a colander and serve at once.

FRIED HOMINY.

Cut cold boiled hominy into small pieces for serving, dip in crumbs, egg and crumbs, and fry in hot cottolene.

BATTERS.

Batters are mixtures of flour and some liquid, and are generally made light by beating in air, or using something to produce carbonic acid gas. For the thin batters, the proportions are one cup of liquid to one cup of flour. A general rule for mixing is to sift flour, salt, and baking powder, if used, into a bowl. Beat the egg well, add the liquid to the egg, pour half of the liquid into the centre of the flour, and gradually work the flour in; beat it till perfectly smooth, then beat in the remainder of the liquid. Do not *stir*, but beat every time before cooking. Every thing should be ready, fire, pans, etc., before starting to mix them, as they should be cooked immediately, that the air, entangled by beating, does not escape. The heat of cooking expands the entangled air, which puffs up the material and makes the mixture light. They should be put into hot, well greased pans, and baked in a hot oven; if cooked on a griddle it should be hot, and rubbed each time all over with a piece of fat salt pork. Do not attempt to do any thing else while you are cooking them, but have everything right at your hand, a hot plate to put them on, and cook them as quickly as possible. Do not put them aside to stand as they should be eaten at once. Never pile but a few on top of each other; serve them and take another plate to serve the next on.

RICE GRIDDLE CAKES.

1 c. cooked rice.   2 eggs.
1 c. milk.   1 tbsp. butter.
½ tsp. salt.   ½ tsp. Cleveland's baking-powder.
Flour enough to make a thin batter.

Beat the eggs well, add the milk and salt, then the rice, and lastly the flour, which has had the baking-powder and salt sifted with it. Use ½ a cup of flour at first and add more if you need it.

HOMINY GRIDDLE CAKES.

Prepare the same as rice cakes.

BUCKWHEAT CAKES.

1 qt. cold water, 1 tsp. salt, 4 c. buckwheat, ½ cake of compressed yeast, dissolved in ¼ c. lukewarm water, 1 tbsp. molasses, ½ tsp. soda. Put the water, salt and buckwheat in a jar, beat thoroughly, add the yeast, mix well, cover, and let stand over night. In the morning stir down, add the soda, dissolved in a very little hot water, beat well, add the molasses, and bake on a hot griddle. The molasses makes them brown better.

PAN CAKES.

2 c. flour.   2 c. milk.
2 ssp. salt.   2 tsp. melted butter.
2 tsp. Cleveland's baking-powder.   1 egg.

Sift the dry ingredients, beat the egg, add the milk and butter, stir into the flour, beat till smooth and pour from the end of the spoon on to a hot, well greased griddle. When the cakes are full of bubbles turn over and brown the other side.

WAFFLES.

1 pt. sifted flour.	½ tsp. salt.
1¼ c. milk.	3 eggs.
1 tsp. Cleveland's baking-powder.	1 tbsp. butter.

Sift the baking-powder and salt with the flour. Beat the yolks of the eggs, add the milk and the melted butter, stir in the flour, beat till smooth; add the well beaten whites last. Grease the waffle iron with fat salt pork and pour into the centre of the iron. Serve with lemon syrup.

YEAST WAFFLES.

1 pt. milk.	⅜ cake compressed yeast.
1 pt. sifted flour.	2 eggs.
½ tsp salt.	½ tbsp. melted butter.

Scald the milk; when lukewarm add the yeast, dissolved in ⅓ c. of lukewarm milk. Stir in the flour with the salt. Beat well and set to rise over night. In the morning add the well beaten eggs, and the butter.

BREAD.

To be able to make good bread is an accomplishment which any woman ought to be proud of, for if it be "the staff of life" it should be the duty of every housekeeper to see that it is a support and a stay, with which to press onward, and not a load, always holding one back. The following extract from a private letter from Mrs. Garfield to her husband may inspire some one to "go and do likewise": "I am glad to tell you that out of all the toil and disappointment of the summer just ended, I have risen up to a victory. . . . . . It came to me one morning when I was making bread. I said to myself, 'Here I am, compelled by an inevitable necessity, to make our bread this summer. Why not consider it a pleasant occupation, and make it so, by trying to see what perfect bread I can make?' It seemed like an inspiration, and the whole of life grew brighter. The very sunshine seemed flowing down through my spirit into the white loaves, and now I believe my table is furnished with better bread than before. . . . . . I need not be the shrinking slave of toil, but it's regal master, making whatever I do yield me it's best fruits."

In order to have our bread sweet and wholesome a slight knowledge of the properties contained in it, and the chemical changes which take place, are necessary.

Wheat is the grain from which we make the most

perfect bread, as it contains a tough, gray, sticky substance, which is called gluten, a large quantity of starch, and more mineral matter than any other grain. The whole wheat grain contains all of these elements, in a larger degree than the fine wheat flour, which has lost some of the nutritious part during the process of grinding. Good flour is absolutely necessary to the making of good bread. None but the best should ever be bought, and the most satisfactory test is to buy a little, give it a fair trial and, if satisfactory, use it. After using many of the brands in the market I can recommend "Pillsbury" as the most thoroughly satisfactory in every way, never having had a failure with it during years of continued use. The next important thing is to have good yeast, the most convenient and reliable being the compressed cakes, one cake being equal to 1 c. of yeast. Yeast is one of the lowest orders of vegetable life, and is a plant of the fungus tribe, to which mold and mildew belong. Like all plants, it needs food, moisture, and warmth, to grow. When the yeast is moistened and put into the flour, it finds the food and conditions adapted to growth; one little cell grows from another, until millions are formed in a few hours. Great care should be taken not to kill the life of the plant at the beginning of the process, by having the liquid too hot. The yeast plant, as it begins to grow, first attacks the starch in the wheat, some of which is changed into sugar; then the sugar is changed into alcohol and carbonic acid gas. This gas tries to escape from the dough and the tenacity and elasticity of the gluten holds it, filling the dough with bubbles. If this is not checked in time, the alcoholic fermentation changes to the acetic, and the dough becomes sour. It is to obtain the carbonic acid gas that we use the yeast; and we knead the dough to break up the large bubbles and make the bread fine grained. As the bread is baked the yeast is killed, the carbonic acid gas tries to escape and so raises the loaf, the starch is cooked and the alcohol passes off. The sweet crust is caused by the decomposition of the starch on the outside, the intense heat changing it to dextrine. That the bread should be perfectly sweet, attention and care must be given to the temperature. The liquid should never be more than lukewarm when the yeast is added, and when first kneaded up, the dough should be kept well covered, out of any draught of cold air, and in a temperature of about 75°. When risen to double its size it should be cut down, as if allowed to "cave in" it is apt to sour. After it has been kneaded into loaves, it is best to leave it in a temperature of 100° until it rises to double its size, then bake at once.

BAKING BREAD.

There are several ways of testing the heat of the oven without using a thermometer; the most reliable one is to put a tablespoonful of flour in the oven, and it should brown in five minutes. The bread will rise in the oven, so it is best not to let it rise too high before baking it. It should not begin to brown until it has been in the oven ten minutes, and should always be placed where the heat will be greatest at the bottom of the pan, causing it to rise before it browns. Should it brown too quickly, protect it with a piece of paper laid over it; and it should be attended to constantly, and after the crust begins to brown, turn carefully, that it may be evenly browned all over. When thoroughly done it will be brown all over, and have a hollow sound when knocked with the knuckles. Remove from the pan as soon as done, tip against something, that the air may reach all sides, and if you want a crisp crust do not cover it. If a soft crust is desired, wrap in a linen cloth. Do not put away until perfectly cold and keep in a clean jar or box. Never keep a cloth in the box; remove all crumbs and stale pieces, and scald out every two or three days.

BREAD MADE WITH WATER.

2 qts. sifted flour.   1½ tbsp. butter, or lard.

1 tsp. salt.   1 pt. boiling water.

¼ cake compressed yeast, dissolved in ½ c. lukewarm water.   ½ tbsp. sugar.

Put the salt, sugar and lard in a bowl, pour on the boiling water, stir well. Dissolve the yeast in the ½ c. lukewarm water, and when liquid in the bowl is lukewarm, add the yeast. Cut in the flour with a knife, adding a cup at a time; as it thickens beat thoroughly with the knife; when thick enough to knead turn out on a well floured board, flour the hands well and knead by drawing the dough farthest from you towards the centre, and press down with the palm of the hand. Continue until the dough is long and narrow, turn half way round and begin kneading again. Knead until it does not stick to the board, put in a greased pan or bowl, cover well, and let rise till double its size. You may not be able to use all of the two quarts of flour at the first kneading. When risen, turn out on a floured board, knead until the large bubbles are all broken up, and using the flour sparingly, shape into loaves, put in a well greased pan, prick with a fork two or three places, cover with a damp cloth, set in a warm place to rise. When risen bake. It should take from 40 to 60 m., according to the sized loaves. By keeping the bread covered with a damp cloth during all the rising, a very delicate and delicious crust is formed.

BREAD MADE WITH MILK.

2 qts. sifted flour.   1 tbsp. butter, or lard.
1 tsp. salt.   1 pt. scalded milk.
¼ cake compressed yeast, dissolved in ½ c. lukewarm milk.   ½ tbsp. sugar.

Proceed the same as for bread made with water.

BREAD WITH POTATOES.

2 qts. sifted flour.   1½ tbsp. butter, or lard.
1 tsp. salt.   1 pt. boiling water.
¼ cake compressed yeast, dissolved in ½ c. lukewarm water.   ½ c. mashed potato.

Proceed the same as for bread made with water, putting the potato in the bowl with the butter, salt, and sugar, and pouring the water on gradually, mashing the potato free from lumps.

GRAHAM BREAD.

1 pt. milk (scalded.)   2 c. white flour.
1 tsp. salt.   ½ c. graham flour (sifted.)
1 tbsp. butter, or lard.   3 tbsp. sugar.
¼ cake compressed yeast, dissolved in ½ c. lukewarm milk.

Prepare as for bread made with water, making a moister dough by using less flour, possibly not all that is given, as flour differs. It is best to set it in the morning, as it sours sooner than white bread, and should be baked in not quite as hot an oven.

ROLLS.

¼ c. lard. 1 tbsp. sugar.
½ tsp. salt. 3½ c. flour.
1 c. scalded milk. ¼ (generous) cake yeast.

Prepare as for bread made with water, kneading very little; set aside in greased bowl covered with damp cloth; when risen, turn out on a slightly floured board, turn over with a knife, so that all may be slightly floured; *do not knead*, roll out ⅓ of inch thick, cut into shape and put in well greased pan, cover with damp cloth, let rise to double their size, in a warm place; bake in an oven that will brown a little flour in one minute. They should bake in 15 m. Turn out of the pan at once, let them lay upside down for 1 m.; serve hot. Be very careful to have no dry flour on rolls or bread when they go in the oven, as they will have a floury look when done. Use very little flour when shaping, and very little on the hands and rolling pin.

TWIN ROLLS.

Prepare as for rolls and cut out two small rounds; spread one with a little melted butter, lay the other on top and bake. The lower one may be made a size larger than the upper one if desired.

CRESCENTS.

Are made by rolling the dough ¼ in. thick, cut

in pieces 4 in. square, then into triangles. Roll up, pulling the point over and under the roll, turning the ends round like a horseshoe.

SWEDISH ROLLS.

When rolled out, spread with soft butter with a knife or pastry brush, sprinkle with a little cinnamon mixed with a little sugar (allow $\frac{1}{2}$ tsp. cinnamon to $\frac{1}{2}$ c. sugar), a little grated lemon rind and a few currants. Roll up like a jelly roll, cut slices off the end $\frac{1}{3}$ of an inch thick, lay the side cut down on a well greased pan, let rise and bake.

WHITE MOUNTAIN ROLLS.

1 pt. milk.	1 tsp. salt.
$\frac{1}{3}$ c. butter.	Whites 2 eggs.
$\frac{1}{4}$ c. sugar.	7 c. flour.

$\frac{1}{3}$ cake compressed yeast dissolved in $\frac{1}{4}$ c. lukewarm water.

Prepare as for rolls, leaving out the eggs. When risen, add the eggs beaten stiff, beat and cut them in with a knife, let rise again, turn out on a floured board, roll out and cut into shapes, put on a well greased pan, not too near together, let rise and bake in a hot oven.

PARKER HOUSE ROLLS.

1 pt. scalded milk.	$\frac{1}{2}$ c. butter.
1 tbsp. sugar. 4 c. flour.	Whites 2 eggs.

$\frac{1}{3}$ cake compressed yeast dissolved in $\frac{1}{4}$ c. lukewarm milk.

Prepare as for rolls. When risen, add the eggs well beaten, cut in well with a knife, knead for a couple of minutes, return to the bowl, cover and let rise, turn out and knead very little, roll out and cut into small rounds, butter half the round, fold over, press the fold, lay on a well greased pan; when risen to double their size bake in a hot oven. Brush over with melted butter as soon as done.

TWISTS.

$\frac{1}{4}$ c. lard.	$\frac{1}{2}$ tsp. salt.
3 c. flour.	1 c. milk.
$\frac{1}{8}$ cake compressed yeast.	$\frac{1}{2}$ tbsp. sugar.

Scald the milk, pour it on to the lard, sugar and salt; when lukewarm add the yeast, which has been dissolved in quarter of a cup of lukewarm water; beat in the flour, cover and set to rise. When risen to double its size, roll out one-quarter of an inch thick, cut into strips one-quarter of an inch wide and four inches long. Brush these over with a little melted butter, make a braid out of three strips and put on a well greased pan not too near together. Cover and let rise till double their size, and bake in a hot oven ten minutes.

CURRANT BUNNS.

1 c. milk, scalded.	1 ssp. salt.
1 tbsp. sugar.	2 c. flour.
1 egg.	$\frac{1}{2}$ c. currants.
2 ssp. cinnamon.	2 tbsp. melted butter.

$\frac{1}{4}$ cake yeast dissolved in $\frac{1}{4}$ c. lukewarm milk.

Pour the milk on to the sugar and salt, beat the egg well and add it; when lukewarm, add the yeast, then cut and beat in the flour. Let rise, well covered; when risen, add the melted butter, currants and cinnamon, beat in thoroughly and let rise again.

When risen turn out, shape into small round cakes and put close together on well greased pan, let rise and bake. Should be served hot.

RAISIN BUNNS.

¼ c. lard. 2 tbsp. sugar.
½ tbsp. salt, 3 c. flour.
1 egg. ¾ c. raisins, stoned.
⅓ cake compressed yeast. 1 c. milk.

Scald the milk, pour it on to the lard, sugar and salt ; when lukewarm add the yeast which has been dissolved in ¼ c. lukewarm water. Cut in the flour and give a thorough beating. Cover with a damp cloth and set to rise. When risen double its size, beat the egg well, and add with the raisins, which have been stoned and cut into quarters. Beat it thoroughly, cover, and set to rise again. When risen again, put by the spoonful into buttered patty pans, cover and stand in a warm place 15 m.; bake in a hot oven 15 m. These may be set at ten A. M. and baked for six o'clock supper.

BISCUITS, GEMS AND MUFFINS.

All quick preparations of hot biscuits are made light by the use of soda and cream of tartar, soda and sour milk, or baking-powder. Baking-powder is a preparation of cream of tartar, which is an acid, and soda, which is an alkali, with a small quantity of corn starch or flour to preserve and keep them. Strong alkalies are corrosive poisons and injure the inside coating of the stomach, but when soda is properly combined with an acid, carbonic acid gas is formed, and the poisonous property is lost, the residue from the union being Rochelle salt. Cream of tartar is very expensive and consequently is freely adulterated with alum or ammonia, very harmful substances, and unless purchased from a reliable chemist is best not used at all; and as great care should be used in combining soda and cream of tartar, that the results may not be injurious to health, it is far better to buy a good, pure baking-powder, which has been carefully prepared by a chemist, than to risk the haphazard measurements of a careless cook. After having carefully and thoroughly tested, in all of my class work, lectures, and at home, the "Cleveland Superior Baking Powder" has never failed to give the best. results. It is more economical, less being needed than other powders; and the food prepared with it keeps moist longer and has a better taste.

Soda may be combined with the lactic acid found in sour milk; the proportion used being 1 level tsp. soda to 1 pt. thick sour milk.

Soda also will unite with the acetic acid contained in molasses, the proportion being 1 level tsp. to 1 c. of molasses, for batters, and ½ tsp. soda to 1 c. molasses, for doughs. All preparations in which soda is combined with an acid, should have, as far as possible, the soda added at the last, and cooked immediately, as moisture hastens the chemical change, and the food should be cooked before the carbonic acid gas escapes, that it may be light.

BISCUITS.

¾ tbsp. lard. ½ tsp. salt.
1 scant c. milk. 1 pt. flour.
2 tsp. Cleveland's baking-powder.

Sift the baking-powder, salt and flour, rub in the lard with the tips of the fingers, moisten with the milk, using a knife to mix with; use only enough milk to make a soft dough. Turn out on a well-floured board, sprinkle a little flour over the top, pat down to ⅓ inch thick with a rolling pin, cut out and put in well-greased pan. Bake in a hot oven about 10 m. Do not have any dry flour on the biscuits when they go in the oven. Cut as economically as possible, that you may have small bits left.

DROP BISCUITS.

2 c. flour.   ½ tsp. salt.
1 tbsp. lard.   1 scant c. milk.
2 tsp. Cleveland's baking-powder.

Sift the salt, baking-powder and flour, rub in the lard with the tips of the fingers, add the milk, cutting in with a knife; mix as little as possible; when all the flour is wet, drop by the teaspoonful on well-buttered pan, putting them far apart that they may be browned all over. These are very quickly made, save the trouble of a board and rolling pin, and are delicious.

GEMS.

2 c. flour.   1 tbsp. melted butter.
1 c. milk.   ½ tsp. salt.
2 tsp. Cleveland's baking-powder.

Sift the flour, salt and baking-powder, add the milk gradually, beating smooth; when all is used, add the butter, pour into hot, buttered gem pans and bake in a hot oven 20 m.

EGG GEMS.

2 c. flour.	2 eggs.
2 c. milk.	$\frac{1}{2}$ tsp. salt.
$\frac{1}{2}$ tbsp. sugar.	2 tbsp. melted butter.

2 tsp. Cleveland's baking-powder.

Sift the flour, salt, baking-powder and sugar. Beat the eggs light (white and yolk together), add the milk, pour into the flour gradually, beating smooth, add the melted butter, give a good beating, pour into piping hot buttered gem pans, and bake in a very hot oven $\frac{1}{2}$ hour. Give a thorough beating each time you fill the pans.

CORN MEAL MUFFINS.

1 c. flour.	1 c. sweet milk (scant.)
$\frac{1}{2}$ c. yellow corn meal.	1 tbsp. butter, melted.
$\frac{1}{4}$ c. sugar.	$\frac{1}{2}$ tsp. salt.
2 tsp. Cleveland's baking-powder.	1 egg.

Sift the flour, meal, salt and baking-powder, add the sugar, beat the egg, add the milk to it, stir into the flour, add the butter, beat well, bake in well-greased gem pans 30 m.

CORN BREAD.

2 c. flour.	2 c. sweet milk (scant.)
1 c. yellow corn meal.	2 tbsp. butter, melted.
$\frac{1}{2}$ c. sugar.	1 tsp. salt.
4 tsp. Cleveland's baking-powder.	2 eggs.

Proceed as for corn meal muffins; bake in a broad, shallow pan, well-greased, in a hot oven for 30 m. Cut in square pieces, being careful to hold the knife perpendicularly, so as not to make the hot bread heavy.

GRAHAM GEMS.

2 c. graham flour, sifted.	2 eggs.
1 c. wheat flour.	$\frac{1}{2}$ tsp. salt.
$\frac{1}{4}$ c. sugar.	$2\frac{1}{2}$ c. milk.
2 tsp. Cleveland's baking-powder.	$\frac{1}{4}$ c. melted butter.

Sift the flour, sugar, salt and baking-powder, beat the eggs, add the milk to them, pour on to the flour gradually, beat till smooth, add the butter and put into piping hot buttered gem pans, and bake about 30 m.

QUICK MUFFINS.

3 c. flour.	$\frac{1}{4}$ tsp. salt.
$2\frac{1}{2}$ c. milk.	$\frac{1}{2}$ tbsp. sugar.
3 level tsp. cottolene.	$1\frac{1}{2}$ tsp. Cleveland's baking-powder.

Sift the flour, salt, baking-powder, and sugar; soften the cottolene. Stir the milk into the flour quickly, add the cottolene, put into small gem pans which have been greased with cottolene and heated on the side of the fire. Bake in a hot oven about 20 m.

BREAKFAST MUFFINS.

3 c. sifted flour.	2 eggs.
2 c. milk.	1 tsp. salt.
3 level tsp. cottolene.	1 tbsp. sugar.
2 tsp. Cleveland's baking-powder.	

Sift the flour, salt, sugar, and baking-powder. Soften the cottolene. Beat the eggs well, add the milk to them, stir into the flour quickly, add the cottolene, and put in hot gem pans, which have been greased with cottolene. Bake 20 m. in hot oven.

MUFFINS.

2 c. flour.　　2 eggs.
¾ c. milk.　　⅓ c. butter, melted.
½ tsp. salt.　　2 tsp. Cleveland's baking-powder.

Sift flour, baking-powder, and salt. Beat the eggs well, add the milk to them; stir in quickly to the flour, add the butter, and bake in hot, well greased muffin pans, in very hot oven, about 15 m.

YEAST MUFFINS.

1 pt. milk, scalded.　　2 eggs.
3 c. sifted flour.　　½ tbsp. sugar.
1 tbsp. butter.　　1 tsp. salt.
½ cake compressed yeast, dissolved in ½ c. lukewarm milk.

Pour the milk on to the butter, salt and sugar; when lukewarm add the yeast, then add the flour; give a thorough beating, set aside to rise over night. In the morning beat the yolks well, add them, then the well beaten whites; let rise 15 m., put into greased pans and bake in the oven 15 m.; or you can bake on griddle on top of the stove.

SALLY LUNN.

2 c. flour.　　2 eggs.
½ tsp. salt.　　¾ c. milk.
2 tsp. Cleveland's baking-powder.　　½ c. melted butter.

Sift the flour, salt, and baking-powder; beat the yolks well, add the milk, stir into the flour, beat till smooth, add the butter, and lastly, the well beaten whites. Do not beat much after the whites are added. Bake in hot, buttered pans, in very hot oven, about 20 m.

SALLY LUNN (with yeast.)

1 c. milk scalded.
½ tsp. salt.
1 tbsp. sugar.
1 tbsp. melted butter.
1 egg.
¼ cake yeast, dissolved in ¼ c. lukewarm milk.
1 c. flour.

Pour the milk on to the salt and sugar; when lukewarm add the yeast; stir in the flour and beat till smooth. Set aside to rise, well covered; when risen, add the egg, well beaten, and the melted butter. Beat well, put in buttered tins, and let rise 15 m.; bake in a hot oven.

EGGS.

Although eggs are a type of perfect food, they are so highly concentrated that many persons cannot eat them, and when improperly cooked they are indigestible for any one. They are very nutritious, and take the place of meat at a much less cost. The white of egg is albumen, and the yolk contains albumen, oil and sulphur. In cooking them remember that albumen hardens at 168°, and never raise the liquid in which they are cooked above that temperature. You may preserve them for some time by coating the shells with anything that will keep out the air; the shells being porous let the water evaporate from the egg, the air enters, and causes decomposition. You may dip them in suet and pack in salt, with the small end downward. They should always have the shells wiped off and be kept in a cool place. Use the dark-shelled ones for anything that you desire well colored, such as sponge cake, custards, etc. They are much richer than the lighter shelled ones.

SOFT BOILED EGG.

Cover the egg with boiling water and stand where the water will simmer for 6 or 10 m., according to the individual taste.

HARD BOILED EGG.

Cover with boiling water and simmer 20 m.

DROPPED EGG.

Toast a round of bread for each egg, butter it and

lay on a hot platter. Fill a frying-pan ⅔ full of boiling water, add a little salt and a very little vinegar. Break each egg carefully into a saucer, and slip the egg into the water. Keep the pan where the water will just simmer. When the white is firm take up one at a time on a skimmer, trim the edges and slip off on to the toast. Shake a very little salt and white pepper over each egg and serve.

SCRAMBLED EGGS.

Beat 2 eggs slightly with a fork, add a scant quarter of a cup of milk, ⅓ tsp. salt, and a little pepper. Put ½ tbsp. butter into a perfectly clean, small, frying-pan; when melted, pour in the egg and cook, stirring all the time with a knife, until the egg is firm, but not hard. Pile on buttered toast, sprinkle a little chopped parsley over and serve hot.

BAKED EGGS.

Cover a buttered dish with seasoned buttered crumbs. Break each egg carefully and put on the dish, and cover with seasoned crumbs. Bake till the crumbs are brown.

OMELET. (Plain.)

2 eggs, 1 tbsp. milk, ¼ tsp. salt, a very little pepper. Beat the eggs well, add the milk, salt and pepper, turn into a hot, buttered frying-pan. Slip a round-bladed knife round the edges as it thickens, and keep the pan turned, that it may be evenly browned. When brown, fold over carefully, letting the part not done pour on to the pan; fold this up on top, put on a hot dish, by holding the dish over the omelet, and turning the frying pan over.

EGGS. 155

OMELET No. 2.

2 eggs.   1 ssp. salt.   1 ssp. pepper.

Beat the yolks with a dover beater till thick and creamy, add the salt and pepper. Beat the whites till stiff and dry, and pour the yolks over them, cutting and folding them in. Do not stir or beat. Butter a small, hot frying-pan, put in by the teaspoonful. Watch and turn the pan that it may cook evenly; when light brown underneath, and you can tell by slipping a knife under and raising a little, put in an oven, or hold a lid over to dry the top, slip a knife under, fold over and turn on to a hot dish. It must be served at once or it will fall.

OMELET No. 3.

Beat the yolks of two eggs till thick, add $\frac{1}{8}$ tsp. salt, $\frac{1}{4}$ ssp. pepper and 1 tbsp. milk. Turn into a hot buttered frying-pan. Beat the whites stiff, and when the omelet is set, pile the whites up and set in the oven a few minutes. Roll over and serve. These may be made in individual ones, and a number of them on a platter look very attractive.

HAM OMELETS.

Prepare as for omelet No. 1, using no salt; when the omelet is almost set, sprinkle with chopped, cooked ham, fold over and serve. You may use any kind of meat you may have.

CREAMY OMELET.

2 eggs, $\frac{1}{4}$ c. milk, $\frac{1}{2}$ tsp. salt, 1 tsp. butter, $\frac{1}{2}$ tbsp. flour, $\frac{1}{2}$ ssp. pepper. Heat the milk, cook the flour and butter, add the hot milk gradually, beat well, set aside to cool. When cold, beat the yolks till

thick and creamy, add the pepper and salt, cut into the cooked milk and flour, beat the whites till stiff, cut in to the other mixture, put by the teaspoonful on a hot, buttered frying-pan. When the under side is brown fold over and serve.

ORANGE OMELET.

2 eggs, 3 tbsp. orange juice and pulp, 3 tbsp. powdered sugar. Separate the eggs; beat the yolks till light and creamy, add the sugar, beat well. Beat the yolks till dry, fold the yolks into the whites. Add the orange juice and pulp, fold lightly, put into a hot, buttered frying-pan, by the teaspoonful. When done, fold over and sprinkle with powdered sugar, and score with a red-hot poker.

OMELET SOUFFLÉ.

Yolks of 2 eggs.   2 heaping tsp. powd. sugar.
Whites of four eggs. $\frac{1}{2}$ tsp. lemon or vanilla extract.

Beat the yolks till thick and creamy, add the sugar gradually, beat the whites stiff, fold the yolks into the whites, cutting them in with a knife; add the flavoring, put into a well-buttered baking dish by the teaspoonful. Cook in a moderate oven about 15 m., till well puffed up and brown, and when a straw comes out clean it is done.

STUFFED EGGS.

Boil 3 eggs 20 m. Cut lengthwise, remove the yolks. Add to them $\frac{1}{2}$ tsp. butter, 2 drops onion juice, half the quantity of deviled ham. Fill the whites, smooth, press together, lay them on the remainder of the yolk mixture on a shallow dish.

Cover with white sauce, sprinkle with large, buttered bread crumbs, and bake till a delicate brown.

BIRD'S NEST.

3 eggs, 3 rounds of toast, 1½ ssp. salt, 3 tbsp. deviled ham. Break the eggs carefully, put the whites in a bowl, and keep each yolk in its own shell by standing the shell up against something. Spread the ham on the toast, heat the whites stiff and heap on the toast, make a hole in the centre, and put one yolk in each hole. Handle the eggs very carefully, so as not to break the yolks. Set in the oven for 3 m. Serve at once.

SPANISH EGGS.

1 c. rice.
6 eggs.
1 tbsp. butter.
1 tbsp. salt.
2 qts. boiling water.
1 c. bread crumbs.

Pick over and wash the rice, put it with the salt into the boiling water and boil till the rice is tender, about thirty minutes. Drain through a colander. Spread the rice on a dish, make small hollows for the eggs, and lay each egg in a hollow. Melt the butter and pour over the crumbs, which should be large, white ones; cover with the crumbs, and bake till the crumbs are brown.

CREAMED EGGS.

1 c. milk, hot.
1 tbsp. butter.
1 tbsp. flour.
¼ tsp. salt.
½ ssp. white pepper.
1 tbsp. parsley.
3 hard-boiled eggs.
Dresden patties or toasted bread cases.

Chop the whites and half of the yolks of the eggs.

Cook the butter, flour, salt and pepper, add the milk gradually, stirring hard, then the eggs and parsley. Fill the cases and press the other half of the egg yolk through a fine sieve on top.

EGGS IN DRESDEN PATTY CASES.

Prepare the cases, poach one egg for each case, trim neatly, slip into the case; put a little salt, pepper and chopped parsley on top of each egg and serve at once.

POACHED EGGS.

Have a shallow pan of boiling water, into which put a little salt. Break each egg carefully into a saucer and slip gently into the water. Draw the pan where the water will just simmer. When the whites are firm, lift up one egg at a time, trim, and lay on buttered toast.

EGGS IN TOMATOES.

Choose round, medium-sized tomatoes Cut off a slice and scoop out some of the tomato; dust a little salt and pepper in the tomato, and put one raw egg in the cavity. Bake in a hot oven till the egg is done; serve on rounds of toast.

EGG WITH CHEESE.

6 eggs.   1 tbsp. butter.
$\frac{1}{4}$ tsp. salt.   spk. cayenne.
3 tbsp. grated Parmesan.

Beat the eggs slightly, add the seasoning; put the butter in an omelet pan; when hot, add the eggs and the cheese, and stir till thick and smooth. Serve on toast.

EGGS FOR BREAKFAST.

Cut slices of stale bread one-and-one-half inch thick. Scoop out the middle, leaving the bottom and sides half an inch thick. Toast the rounds, put a raw egg in the centre of each, and bake in the oven till the egg is set.

SALADS.

To have a delicious salad, everything used for it should be very cold, the lettuce or greens fresh and crisp, and the dressing perfectly smooth. Keep everything on the ice and never mix mayonnaise with the salad, until just before using. You may prepare a French dressing and marinate the salad with it, an hour or so before it is needed. Lay the lettuce in ice water for an hour or two, dry thoroughly and carefully on a towel. Never cut lettuce with a knife, but pull it apart with the fingers, reserving the small leaves from the heart to decorate with. Do not use any leaves that are discolored or wilted. Use only the white, crisp part of celery, saving the rest for stews or soup. Keep it on the ice until served.

MAYONNAISE.

1 tbsp. mustard.
1 " sugar.
¼ ssp. Cayenne.
1 tsp. salt.
1 pt. salad oil.
¼ c. vinegar.
½ lemon.
1 c. whipped cream.
Yolks of 3 raw eggs.

Cut an onion in half, rub round the bowl once, put in the dry ingredients, add the yolks, beat with a dover beater till thick. Add the oil, a few drops at a time, beating hard all the time, and when the mixture becomes too thick, add a few drops of vinegar to thin it; continue with the oil until all is used; add the vinegar and lemon last. Just before serving add the whipped cream. Should it curdle, sometimes a little vinegar will bring it smooth again; if this fails, take the yolk of another raw egg, beat well in another bowl and add gradually the curdled mixture to it, beating hard all the time. This never fails to bring it back. The cause of its curdling, is either that the oil is added too fast, or that the ingredients are not cold. Keep the eggs and oil on the ice, and if possible stand the bowl in which you make it, in a pan of ice.

FRENCH DRESSING.

1 ssp. salt. 1 tbsp. vinegar. 3 tbsp. oil.
½ ssp. white pepper.

Mix the salt and pepper, add a little oil. Stir and add a little vinegar, and then the rest of the oil.

BOILED DRESSING.

1 tsp. mustard.	2 tbsp. sugar.
2 " salt.	½ c. vinegar.
¼ ssp. cayenne.	1 c. cream.
2 tbsp. clarified butter.	3 eggs.

Mix the dry ingredients, moisten with the vinegar and pour on to the beaten egg, stirring well. Add the cream. Clarify the butter by melting, and after letting the salt settle, pour off the liquid and add to the dressing. Place the bowl in a pan of boiling water, and stir constantly till it thickens like custard. Remove from the fire and strain and cool. The acid of the vinegar does not act as quickly on the cream as it does on milk. This dressing is very delicious, and for those who cannot take oil, is a very good substitute.

MAYONNAISE TARTAR

Prepare the same as for mayonnaise without the cream, and add 1 tbsp. each of chopped olives, capers, pickles, and parsley.

POTATO SALAD.

3 good sized potatoes. 2 tbsp. chopped parsley.
1 cold boiled beet. 1 small onion.
1 hard boiled egg. Salt and pepper.
French dressing.

Have the potato boiled and cold, cut in thin slices. Cut the beet in thin slices, then with a fancy cutter cut into shapes. Chop the onion *very* fine. Put a layer of potato on a dish, then a few pieces of beet, sprinkle with dressing and a little onion and parsley; repeat till all is used. Decorate with parsley and egg, the yolk and white chopped separately.

LETTUCE SALAD.

Break off the leaves, wash carefully and lay in cold water, ice water is best, till ready to serve. Take up the leaves, shake carefully and dry gently between two towels. Arrange in a salad bowl, with the small leaves in the centre, and serve with French dressing.

CHICKEN SALAD.

Remove skin, fat, gristle and bones from cold cooked chicken, and cut into small cubes. Marinate with a French dressing and set in the refrigerator for three hours. Clean and cut up two-thirds as much white celery as you have chicken, wash and put in ice water till needed. Allow 1½ cups of mayonnaise to 1 qt. of salad. Just before serving drain, and dry the celery thoroughly, add the chicken and mix a little of the mayonnaise with it. Put in a salad bowl on a bed of crisp lettuce leaves, cover the top with the mayonnaise, smoothing it with a silver knife; garnish with the small white celery leaves and olives.

LOBSTER SALAD.

The meat of two boiled lobsters weighing 2½ lbs. each, the tender leaves of two or three small heads of lettuce, 1½ c. mayonnaise. Cut the lobster meat into dice, season with French dressing, lay on the ice for 3 hours. Wash the lettuce carefully and lay in ice water for 2 hours. When ready to serve, drain and dry the lettuce on a towel, pull apart the larger leaves with the fingers, holding gently so as not to wilt them; mix ½ c. mayonnaise with it, and put on a bed of lettuce leaves, with the rest of the mayonnaise spread over the top. Decorate with the small claws.

VEGETABLE SALAD.

1 qt. cold boiled potatoes.	1 tbsp. chopped onion.
1 c. " " beets.	½ c. " celery.
½ c. " " carrots.	2 hard boiled eggs.
1 tbsp. chopped parsley.	French dressing, twice the recipe.

Cut the vegetables into cubes or fancy shapes; sprinkle with 1 tsp. salt, ½ tsp. pepper. Chop the onion very fine and add to the French dressing. Mix the vegetables in alternate layers, rub a little of the yolk of the egg through a fine sieve over each layer, and sprinkle the French dressing over. Decorate with a border of chopped white of egg, parsley and the yolk rubbed through a sieve.

EGG SALAD.

Boil 3 eggs 20 m., put on ice. When ready to serve chop the yolks and whites separately. Make a bed of water cresses, press the yolk through a fine strainer in the centre, surround it with the whites, sprinkle French dressing over the whole.

MARGUERITE SALAD.

Cut whites of hard boiled eggs into small pieces to resemble petals. Arrange in wreaths on flat leaves of lettuce, using one leaf for one wreath; moisten the yolks with a little boiled dressing, put through a strainer into the centre of the wreaths. Serve with boiled dressing.

TOMATO SALAD.

Pour boiling water over small, round tomatoes, remove the skins and lay on the ice. When ready to serve, put one tomato on a leaf of lettuce, cut off a very little bit of the top; put a tsp. of mayonnaise on the top and serve.

TOMATO BASKETS.

Choose round tomatoes of medium size. With a small knife make baskets with handles; scoop out the tomato from the basket, and fill the baskets with cubes of raw tomato and small pieces of lettuce. Put a tsp. of mayonnaise on top of each, tie the handles with a ribbon, and serve on bed of greens.

SWEETBREAD SALAD.

2 prepared sweetbreads.   2 tsp. oil.
½ tsp. salt.   ⅛ ssp. white pepper.
2 " vinegar.   ½ c. cooked peas.
        ⅓ c. mushrooms, quartered.

Cut the sweetbreads into dice. Mix the salt, pepper and a little vinegar; add a little oil and a little vinegar till all are used. Mix it with the sweetbreads, peas and mushrooms. Just before serving mix a little mayonnaise with it, and serve in lettuce with mayonnaise on top.

SANDWICHES.

The bread should be fine grained, at least twelve hours old; the knife very sharp and the butter soft. Cut the crust off the loaf, butter each slice very slightly before cutting off the loaf. Be careful to have the slices as thin as possible, and of even thickness. Have the paste soft so that it may not break the bread when spreading on. Butter the bread all over but very slightly, spread with a very thin layer of paste; put on another slice of bread which has been buttered slightly, press together and cut into triangles. Pile up on a plate, cover with a damp napkin and keep in a cool place till used. Any kind of cold meat, using a little of the fat, may be chopped to a fine paste, well seasoned and used. Use a little mustard with ham and tongue.

CELERY SANDWICHES.

Butter very thin slices of bread, chop crisp white celery fine, season well with salt and pepper and lay between the slices.

SALAD SANDWICHES.

Chop cold bits of turkey, chicken or lobster very fine. Mix a very little mayonnaise with the meat. Put a lettuce leaf on a very thin slice of bread, not buttered; then a little salad, another leaf of lettuce, and bread again. They may be wrapped in oil paper for picnics or traveling.

FRENCH SANDWICHES.

Purchase at a first-class baker's what are called finger rolls. Split and remove most of the inside. Butter the inside very slightly, fill with any mixture you desire; chopped ham, tongue, chicken or salad of any kind. If salad is used, do not butter the rolls, and have the pieces of meat, lettuce or celery very small. Tie the rolls with different colored ribbons.

CHEESE SANDWICHES.

3 eggs, 1 tbsp. cheese, grated, 1 level tbsp. butter, 1 spk. cayenne, a little grated tongue or ham.

Beat the eggs, put the butter into a frying-pan, add the eggs, cayenne and cheese, stir over the fire till it thickens; season with a little salt; if the ham be very salt do not use any. Spread the paste on rounds of thin bread, either toasted or fried, sprinkle the ham or tongue over it, and serve. These are very nice for Sunday night tea.

HAM AND CHICKEN SANDWICHES.

Chop equal parts of cold roast or boiled chicken and ham, or veal and ham, *very fine;* put in a frying-pan with enough veal or chicken gravy to make a paste. Season with salt, pepper and a very little cayenne. Cook five minutes, spread out to cool. When cool spread between thin slices of buttered bread.

GINGER SANDWICHES.

Cut candied ginger into thin shavings and lay between very thin slices of bread and butter. Use only one thin layer of ginger in each sandwich.

CROQUETTES.

Croquettes are mixtures of a thick white sauce with cooked meat, fish, grains and vegetables. They can be made without the sauce, but are not as delicate. Have the material as soft as can be molded, and form by putting a tablespoonful of the mixture on to a board covered with fine sifted, seasoned bread crumbs. Roll carefully into a ball, letting none of the crumbs get inside, but a thin coating outside. Hold the fingers together and press and roll the ball on the board till like a cylinder.

Take the croquette gently in the hand, flatten one end on the board, turn the hand over and flatten the other end. Lay on a corner of the board until all are done. Beat one egg, yolk and white, slightly; add 2 tbsp. cold water to it (this is to economize on the egg); put one croquette in and cover with egg by dipping the egg up over it with a spoon or knife, being very careful not to touch the croquette. See that all the bubbles of the egg are broken, and the croquette have a thorough coating of egg, as if there is one spot not covered with the egg the croquette will burst or become fat soaked. It is the albumen of the egg that will harden and make the crust, to prevent the fat from entering. Remove the croquette from the egg by slipping a broad knife under. Put on a board thickly covered with crumbs and cover with crumbs the second time. Dip the frying basket in the hot fat, lay on a plate and put a few in care-

CROQUETTES.

fully, not allowing them to touch each other, and not putting too many in at a time, as they will chill the fat. Test the fat every time before putting them in. It should brown a piece of bread in 40 seconds. Put the basket in slowly and do not raise it until the croquettes are done. They ought to brown in one minute. When done, lift the basket up, drain well over the fat, remove the croquettes on to brown paper. Never put the material for croquettes in a very cold place, as they are apt to burst if at all cold when put in the fat.

THICK CREAM SAUCE FOR CROQUETTES.

1 pt. hot cream.
2 level tbsp. butter.
¾ tsp. celery salt.
A few drops of onion juice.
Speck of cayenne.
4 heaping tbsp. flour.
½ tsp. salt.
½ ssp. white pepper.
2 tbsp. lemon juice.
1 tbsp. chopped parsley.

Prepare as for white sauce, adding the lemon juice after removing from the fire. It should be very thick and mixed while hot with the other ingredients for the croquettes. You may use milk instead of cream, with rounded tablespoonfuls of butter.

CHICKEN CROQUETTES.

To one pint of cooked chicken allow ¾ pt. thick cream sauce. Remove all skin, fat and gristle from the chicken, chop as fine as meal, add the sauce, 1 ssp. mace, a dash of nutmeg, beat well; taste, and see if more salt or pepper is needed, set aside to cool. When cool shape into croquettes, roll in crumbs, egg and crumbs, and fry in hot cottolene.

LOBSTER CROQUETTES.

1 pt. lobster meat. $1\frac{1}{4}$ c. thick cream sauce.
1 ssp. mustard.   1 spk. cayenne.

Chop the meat as fine as meal, add the sauce and seasoning, cool, shape into croquettes, roll in crumbs, egg and crumbs, and fry in hot cottolene.

LOBSTER CUTLETS.

Prepare the same as for croquettes; when the mixture is cool, grease a cutlet-mold with a pastry brush dipped in melted butter; fill the mold with fine bread crumbs, throw them out, letting all adhere to the butter that will. Fill the mold with the cutlet mixture, smooth with a knife, turn out on a board covered with crumbs, cover with egg and crumbs again. Do not butter the mold except the first time, but fill with crumbs each time before using. Fry in hot cottolene. Put a small claw in the end of the cutlet.

CODFISH CROQUETTES.

2 cups cold cooked codfish, 1 pt. thick cream sauce. Flake the fish very fine, add the sauce, $\frac{1}{4}$ ssp. cayenne, $\frac{1}{4}$ tsp. lemon juice, beat well; when cool, shape, roll in crumbs, egg and crumbs, and fry in hot cottolene.

SALMON CROQUETTES.

One pound of cold cooked salmon, or $\frac{3}{4}$ of can. Free the salmon from bones and oil, pick very fine with two forks, add 1 pt. thick cream sauce, stir well; add $\frac{1}{4}$ ssp. cayenne, $\frac{1}{4}$ tsp. lemon juice, few drops of onion juice, and salt if needed, set aside to cool; shape, roll in crumbs, egg and crumbs, and fry in hot cottolene.

SWEETBREAD CROQUETTES.

1½ c. thick cream sauce.   ½ c. warm boiled rice.
1 prepared sweetbread.   ½ can mushrooms.
Salt and pepper, if needed.

Cut the sweetbreads and mushrooms into very small pieces, add the rice and enough sauce to make it soft enough to be handled. Taste it, and see if more seasoning is needed; set aside to cool, shape into croquettes, roll in crumbs, egg and crumbs, and fry in hot cottolene.

POTATO CROQUETTES.

1 c. boiled potato.   ¼ tsp. salt.
½ tbsp. butter.   ¼ "   celery salt.
½ tsp. chopped parsley.   ¼ ssp. white pepper.
1 egg.   1 spk. cayenne.
2 drops onion juice.

Add the seasoning to the hot mashed potato, beat very light, add the beaten egg; when cool, shape, roll in crumbs, egg and crumbs, and fry in hot cottolene.

RICE CROQUETTES.

½ c. rice.   1 pt. hot water.
½ tsp. salt.   1 egg.
1 tbsp. butter.   ½ c. cold meat, chopped fine.

Cook the rice in the water with the salt until quite soft, add the egg, well beaten, the butter; mix well and add the meat. When cold, shape, roll in crumbs, egg and crumbs, and fry in hot cottolene.

CORNED-BEEF CROQUETTES OR BALLS.

Chop one cup of cold cooked corned-beef very fine, add ½ c. hot mashed potato, beat well, season highly with a little salt, pepper, made mustard, and cayenne;

put in a few drops of onion juice, add one well beaten egg. Shape into croquettes or round balls, roll in crumbs, egg and crumbs, and fry in hot cottolene.

FRITTER BATTER.

Yolks of 2 eggs.
⅓ c. milk.
1 tbsp. butter.
1 ssp. salt.
1 c. flour.
Whites of 2 eggs.

Beat the yolks till thick, add the milk and the salt, then add the butter, melted, then the flour. Beat till smooth, and add the well beaten whites last. If used for fruit, add 1 tsp. sugar; if for fish or meat, add 1 tbsp. lemon juice. Beat well each time. Can be kept for several days.

GAME FRITTERS.

Stew the bones and meat till quite tender, remove all skin and gristle, add a few mushrooms, chopped fine, season well with salt, pepper, and cayenne. Allow 1 c. of meat to the fritter batter, beat well and drop by the spoonful into hot cottolene, and fry till golden brown.

OYSTER FRITTERS.

Salt and pepper each oyster, let stand 20 m. Dip each one into the fritter batter and fry in hot cottolene.

CLAM FRITTERS.

Drain and chop fine 25 clams. Drain again and add to the fritter batter. Drop by the spoonful into hot cottolene and fry till brown. You may use the liquor for making the batter if you wish a very strong taste.

CORN FRITTERS.

Add 1 c. corn to the fritter batter. Prepare the

corn by scoring down through the kernels and pressing out with the back of a knife. Drop by the spoonful into hot cottolene and fry till delicate brown.

APPLE FRITTERS.

Core, pare, and slice whole apples, leaving the hole made by the core in the centre, and have the slices $\frac{1}{3}$ inck thick. Mix $\frac{1}{4}$ tsp. ground cinnamon with $\frac{1}{2}$ c. sugar, squeeze a little lemon juice on the slices, sprinkle with the cinnamon and sugar, let stand for 20 m. Dip each slice in the batter and fry in hot cottolene about 4 m. Serve with foamy sauce.

ORANGE FRITTERS.

Divide the orange into sections, remove the thin skin with scissors, dip each section into the fritter batter and fry in hot cottolene. Serve with orange sauce.

PUDDINGS AND DESSERTS.

All puddings in which the milk has to be scalded should be made in a double boiler, as the milk is likely to burn before it is hot enough. When eggs are added to hot milk, the milk should always be poured on to the eggs slowly, stirring the eggs all the time, and then returned to the fire, and stirred constantly till cooked. If you pour the eggs into the milk it is apt to harden in lumps. Should you curdle the eggs and milk by cooking too long, you can sometimes bring it smooth again by beating at once with a dover beater.

SOFT CUSTARD.

2 c. milk.   2 tbsp. sugar.
3 eggs.   1 tsp. flavoring.

Scald the milk in a double boiler; when the bubbles are all over the top of the milk, beat the eggs, add the sugar, beat again, pour the hot milk slowly over the eggs, stirring all the time; return to the double boiler, and stir till it coats the spoon and is thick as cream. Remove at once, as it will curdle, strain, and set aside to cool. Add the flavoring when cold; it evaporates the alcohol in the flavoring to add to a hot liquid, and is therefore extravagant.

FLOATING ISLAND.

1 pt. milk.   2 tbsp. gran. sugar.
3 eggs.   1 tsp. flavoring.
3 tbsp. powdered sugar.

Scald the milk in a double boiler, separate the eggs,

beat the yolks well, add the gran. sugar, pour the milk on to the eggs, stirring well, return to the double boiler and cook till thick as cream, stirring all the time. Strain, and when cold add the flavoring. Whip the whites till stiff, add the powdered sugar gradually, pour the custard in a dish and pile the whites up in spoonfuls on top.

FRUIT CUSTARD.

Make floating island, put slices of sponge cake, spread with jam, in the bottom of a glass dish, pour the custard over them and heap on the whites.

CHOCOLATE CUSTARD.

Make the floating island; just before straining the custard add to it one square of W. Baker & Co.'s No. 1 chocolate; strain, when cold, pile up the beaten whites on the top. Use vanilla flavoring.

BAKED CUSTARD.

1 qt. milk.   6 tbsp. sugar.
4 eggs.   1 ssp. salt.   1 tsp. flavoring (vanilla.)

Scald the milk, separate the eggs, add the sugar and the salt, beat well, pour the milk over the eggs slowly, stirring all the time, beat the whites, stir in lightly, add the flavoring, put into deep dish or cups, set in a pan of hot water. Bake about 30 m., until the custard is firm and shakes like jelly.

ORANGE CUSTARD.

1 qt. milk.   1½ tbsp. cornstarch.
3 eggs.   ½ ssp. salt.
3 tbsp. gran. sugar.   3 tbsp. powd. sugar.

Mix the cornstarch to a smooth paste, with ¼ c. cold milk. Scald the rest of the milk in a double boiler. Separate the eggs, beat the yolks, add the cornstarch and pour the scalded milk over them, stirring well. Return to the fire, cook for 5 m., set aside to cool. Cut up six oranges into small pieces, removing all the seeds and tough membrane; unless quite sweet sprinkle with sugar; when ready to serve pour the custard over the oranges and pile the whites, which have been beaten to a stiff froth, and the powd. sugar, added slowly, on top of the oranges. Everything should be very cold in this dish.

APPLE CUSTARD.

Prepare the same as for orange custard and pour over stewed apples. See directions for stewing apples.

LEMON BREAD PUDDING.

1 qt. milk.
1 pt. fine bread crumbs.
4 eggs.
1 tbsp. butter.
1 c. gran. sugar.
1 c. powdered sugar.
Grated rind and juice of 1 lemon.

Separate the eggs, beat the yolks, set the whites in a cool place. Add the gran. sugar to the yolks, then the milk, bread crumbs and grated rind; bake in the oven about half an hour. Remove from the oven, beat the whites stiff, add the powd. sugar slowly, add the lemon juice, pile on top and stand in the oven with the door open for 20 m. Turn, so that all may be evenly browned. You may improve this pudding by spreading jam or preserves over it before putting the whites on.

CHOCOLATE CUSTARDS.

4 c. milk.
1 c. sugar.
2 sq. W. Baker & Co.'s chocolate.
$\frac{1}{2}$ tsp. vanilla.
4 tsp. cornstarch (level).
4 eggs.

Scald the milk, grate the chocolate, put the chocolate and the sugar in the milk. Beat the yolks of the eggs. Mix the cornstarch with a little cold milk and add it to the eggs; pour the milk over the eggs, return to the fire, and cook till it thickens : about 5 m., stirring all the time. When cold, add the flavoring and put in small glasses. Beat the whites of the eggs stiff, add 2 tbsp. powd. sugar, and heap on the top of the pudding.

TAPIOCA CUSTARD.

4 tbsp. tapioca.   2 c. cold water.
4 c. milk.   3 eggs.
1 tsp. vanilla.   ½ ssp. salt.   1¼ c. sugar.

Soak the tapioca in the water 5 h. Scald the milk, add the tapioca and the salt. Beat the yolks of the eggs and the sugar; when the tapioca is hot, add the yolks, stirring constantly, and cook for 2 m. like custard, stirring all the time. Turn out into a bowl, add the whites, which have been beaten stiff, and fold them in gently. Put 1 tsp. strawberry jam in a small glass; when the tapioca is cold, flavor it, and fill the glasses. Serve in the glasses, very cold. This is a very delicious dessert.

CUSTARD TIMBALES.

Yolks 3 eggs.   ¾ c. scalded milk.
1 ssp. salt.   1 tbsp. sugar.

Beat the yolks and the sugar, add the milk and salt; bake in small, buttered timbale molds set in a pan of hot water, from 20 to 30 m. Set away in the molds till cold and hard, and serve with caramel sauce. Both the pudding and the sauce should be very cold.

FRENCH BREAD PUDDING.

1 pt. milk. Thin slices of bread and butter.
2 eggs. 2 tbsp. gran. sugar.
½ tsp. vanilla. 2 " powd. sugar.
¼ c. raisins.

Butter a medium-sized shallow tin pan. Stone the raisins and cut in half, lay in the pan. Cover with one layer of very thin slices of bread and butter. Beat the yolks of the eggs, lay the whites aside in a cool place, add the gran. sugar to the yolks, pour the milk over them, add the vanilla, stir well, pour over the bread. Bake until a delicate brown, remove from the oven; beat the whites stiff, add the powd. sugar gradually, spread on the top, and bake 15 m. in a cool oven, turning often, that it may be evenly browned. You may spread jelly over the bread just before putting on the whites.

CREAMED RICE PUDDING.

½ c. rice. 1 qt. milk.
½ c. sugar. 1 ssp. salt.
½ nutmeg.

Soak the rice in the milk 2 h.; add the salt and sugar, grate the nutmeg over the top. Bake in a moderate oven 2 hours, until the milk is almost absorbed.

RICE CUSTARD.

Fill small glasses two-thirds full of cooked rice. Make a custard with 3 c. milk, yolks 4 eggs, 3 tbsp. sugar, a speck of salt, and ½ tsp. vanilla. Pour the custard while hot over the rice. Set away till very cold. When ready to serve, whip the whites, add 3 tbsp. powd. sugar, and pile on the top. You may add a layer of preserve before putting on the whites.

APPLE MERINGUE.

Core, pare and bake four medium-sized apples till tender, but not broken, putting a little bit of sugar and grated lemon peel in the centre of each apple. Beat the yolks of 3 eggs, add 3 tbsp. sugar, spk. of salt; add 1 pt. scalded milk, pour over the apples. Bake till the custard is firm. Remove from the oven, beat the whites stiff, add gradually 3 tbsp. powd. sugar, a few drops of lemon juice, pile on the top, and put in a cool oven 15 m.

SCALLOPED APPLE.

$\frac{1}{4}$ c. sugar. $\frac{1}{3}$ c. butter.
1 ssp. cinnamon.   2 c. soft bread crumbs.
1 lemon rind, grated.   3 c. sliced apple.

Mix sugar, cinnamon and lemon rind. Melt the butter and pour it over the bread crumbs, tossing them with a fork. Butter a pudding dish, put in a layer of crumbs, then a layer of apple, sprinkle with the sugar, then a layer of crumbs, apple and sugar, reserving $\frac{3}{4}$ c. crumbs for the top. Put in the oven, cover with a pan, that the crumbs may not brown before the apples are done; bake 20 m.; remove the pan, brown the crumbs, and serve at once.

APPLE COMPOTE.

Add to 1 pt. boiling water 1 c. sugar, 1 strip lemon rind. Boil 5 m. Core and pare six apples, put in the boiling syrup, cover, and boil till a straw passes through easily. Boil gently, or they will break. Remove, fill the cores with orange marmalade, boil the syrup 5 m. longer, and pour around the apples. Serve cold.

COTTAGE PUDDING.

1 heaping cup flour. $\frac{1}{3}$ c. sugar.
$\frac{1}{4}$ tsp. salt. $1\frac{1}{2}$ tsp. melted butter.
1 egg. $\frac{1}{2}$ c. milk.
    1 tsp. Cleveland's baking-powder.

Sift the dry ingredients, beat the egg, add the milk, then the butter, and stir into the flour. Bake in small pans about 15 m., or in one shallow pan 30 m. Grease the pans with butter, and serve hot with lemon sauce.

CHOCOLATE PUDDING.

Yolks 4 eggs. $\frac{1}{2}$ box gelatine (Cox's).
1 qt. milk.   1 tsp. vanilla flavoring.
1 c. sugar.   Whites 4 eggs.
    $\frac{1}{4}$ cake W. Baker & Co.'s chocolate.

Soak the gelatine in $\frac{1}{2}$ c. milk 2 h. Scald the remainder of the milk in a double boiler, beat the yolks of the eggs, add half the sugar, pour on the hot milk, stirring all the time, return to the fire and cook till thick as cream, stirring well. Remove from the fire, add the gelatine, remainder of the sugar and the chocolate, which has been cut up and melted; strain, when cold, add the vanilla. Set in a pan of ice, stir occasionally; when it begins to thicken add the whites, beaten stiff, and beat with a wire spoon till stiff enough to drop. Dip a mold in cold water, pour the mixture in, and set away to cool. Serve very cold, with a cold custard, made with the yolks of 3 eggs, 1 pt. milk, $\frac{1}{2}$ c. sugar, $\frac{1}{4}$ ssp. salt, 1 tsp.

vanilla. This is a most delicious pudding, and can be made on Saturday for Sunday.

SPONGE PUDDING.

⅛ c. sugar.
¼ c. flour.
1 c. milk.
⅛ c. butter.
Yolks 3 eggs.
Whites 3 eggs.

Mix the flour and sugar with a little cold milk, scald the rest of the milk and stir the flour into it. Cook 8 m., stirring well; add the butter; when cool, add the well beaten yolks, then the whites, beaten stiff. Do not beat much after adding the whites. Bake in buttered cups, placed in hot water, in a hot oven, about 30 m. When a straw comes out clean it is done. Serve with orange sauce.

BAKED HUCKLEBERRY PUDDING.

¾ c. butter.
2 c. sugar.
1 tsp. cinnamon.
1 tsp. nutmeg.
3 c. flour.
4 eggs.
1¼ c. milk.
1 qt. fresh huckleberries.
2 tsp. Cleveland's baking-powder.

Cream the butter, add the sugar gradually, add the well-beaten yolks; sift the baking-powder with the flour and the spices, and add a little at a time, alternating with a little milk Add the well-beaten whites; lastly, the berries, being very careful not to break them as you fold them in. Bake in shallow, well-greased tin, or in small gem pans. Serve with foamy sauce.

BOILED HUCKLEBERRY PUDDING.

2 qts. berries.
1 pt. molasses.
Flour to make a stiff dough.
1 level tsp. soda, dissolved in ½ c. hot water.

Dissolve the soda, add it to the molasses, add a little flour, then the berries, stirring gently, then enough flour to make a stiff dough, put in buttered mold, steam 3½ h. Serve with creamy sauce.

SUET PUDDING.

1 ssp. salt.   Cold water to make a soft dough.
1 pt. flour.   ½ c. chopped beef suet.
1½ tsp. Cleveland's baking-powder.

Sift the flour, baking-powder and salt, add the suet and mix well. Add the cold water gradually; put into a well-greased mold, filling to within an inch of the top. Cover with greased paper and steam 2 h. for a mold, 1 h. for cups. Serve with foamy sauce. Use kidney suet for all suet puddings.

GINGER SUET PUDDING.

1 pt. flour.   ½ c. chopped beef suet.
1 ssp. salt.   ¾ c. molasses.
Cold water to make soft   1½ tsp. Cleveland's bak-
  dough.   ing-powder.
1½ tbsp. ground ginger.

Proceed as for suet pudding, using the molasses first, and then enough water to make a stiff dough. Serve with foamy sauce.

FRUIT SUET PUDDING.

Make the same as plain suet pudding, and add to the dry ingredients,

¾ c. currants.   ¾ c. sugar.
¾ c. raisins.   ½ nutmeg.
½ c. sliced citron.   1½ tsp. cinnamon.
2 ssp. cloves.   3 ssp. mace.

Serve with foamy sauce.

CABINET PUDDING.

Yolks 3 eggs.   1 c. fruit.
3 tbsp. sugar.   3 pts. stale sponge cake.
3 c. milk (scalded.) $\frac{1}{2}$ ssp. salt.

Sprinkle the fruit around a well-buttered melon mold, reserving half of it to sprinkle through the cake. Break up the cake and fill the mold, putting in a little fruit now and then. Beat the eggs, sugar, salt; add the milk and pour over the cake. Let it stand 1 h. Steam it $1\frac{1}{4}$ h. Serve with lemon, or creamy sauce. You may use for the cup of fruit, raisins, currants, citron, candied cherries, and candied rhubarb. The rhubarb gives a bright green color, that is very attractive. Some caterers call it angelica.

SWEDISH PUDDING.

$1\frac{1}{2}$ c. milk.   3 eggs. $\frac{1}{2}$ can apricots.
2 tbsp. flour. $\frac{1}{2}$ tsp. vanilla flavoring.
$\frac{1}{2}$ tbsp. butter. $\frac{1}{2}$ " almond "
3 tbsp. powd. sugar.   2 tbsp. gran. sugar.

Scald 1 c. milk; rub the flour to a smooth paste in $\frac{1}{2}$ c. milk, add the yolks of the eggs, and the sugar; pour on the scalded milk; cook 10 m., stirring all the time; add the butter, and when cool add the flavoring. Put in a dish, cover with the apricots, and decorate with the whites of the eggs, beaten to a stiff froth, and the powd. sugar, added gradually. Squeeze this through a paper cornucopia, with a hole in the end. Place in the oven 10 m. Serve cold, with the syrup from the apricots.

APPLE SNOW BALLS.

$\frac{1}{2}$ c. rice. $\frac{1}{2}$ tsp. salt.
2 apples.   1 c. boiling water.

Pick over and wash the rice, and put it with the salt and boiling water into the top of the double boiler. Boil rapidly 10 m., place over hot water and steam 15 m. Have four small pudding cloths of cheese cloth, ⅓ of a yard square. Dip in boiling water and wring out. Place over small bowl, cover with rice, ¼ in. thick; core, pare, and halve the apples, place half an apple in centre of each cloth, put a little rice on top, draw the cloth together, being careful to cover the apple with the rice, tie up tight and steam 30 m. Turn out and serve with lemon sauce.

SNOW BALLS.

3 eggs.	3 tbsp. cold water.
1 c. sugar.	Grated rind 1 lemon.
1 c. sifted flour.	1½ tbsp. lemon juice.

1 tsp. Cleveland's baking-powder.

Beat the yolks till very light, add the sugar gradually, beat well, add the lemon juice, rind and water; sift the flour and baking-powder, add to the mixture, beat well; lastly, fold in the whites, which have been beaten stiff. Steam in well-buttered earthen cups for 30 m. When done, roll in powdered sugar, and serve with strawberry sauce.

MOCK PLUM PUDDING (Baked.)

1 qt. milk.	¼ lb. suet, chopped fine.
3 eggs.	¼ lb. currants.
1 level tsp. soda.	½ lb. raisins.
¼ c. hot water.	1¾ c. fine bread crumbs.
1 tbsp. mixed spice.	½ c. molasses.

⅛ lb. citron, cut fine.

Beat the eggs, add the milk; sift the bread crumbs and spice together, add them to the milk, add the suet, fruit, and molasses, and lastly, the soda, dissolved in the hot water. Bake 1½ h. Serve with hard sauce.

SNOW PUDDING.

¼ box Nelson's gelatine.   1 c. boiling water.
1 c. gran. sugar.   ¼ c. lemon juice.
          Whites 3 eggs.

Soak the gelatine in ¼ c. cold water 2 h. Add the boiling water; when the gelatine is dissolved, add the sugar and lemon juice. Strain and set in a pan of ice. Stir occasionally, and when it begins to harden add the whites, beaten stiff, and beat all with a wire spoon till light and stiff. Put in a mold, wet with cold water, and serve very cold, with a soft custard or chocolate sauce.

ORANGE CHARLOTTE.

¼ box Nelson's gelatine.   Juice 1 lemon.
¼ c. cold water.   1 c. orange juice and pulp.
⅓ c. boiling water.   Whites 3 eggs.
1 c. sugar.   Grated rind of ¼ orange.

Soak the gelatine in the cold water 2 h. Add the boiling water; when dissolved, add the sugar, stir till dissolved, add the lemon juice, strain, and set in a pan of ice water. Stir occasionally; when cold, add the orange juice and pulp, and when it begins to thicken add the whites, which have been beaten stiff, and beat all with a wire spoon until stiff. Pour into a 1 qt. charlotte russe mold, which has been lined with orange sections. Set away to harden, and serve with whipped cream piled around and on top of the charlotte.

PUDDINGS AND DESSERTS.

ORANGES FILLED WITH JELLY.

Cut a small round hole in the end of the orange. With a small spoon scoop out the inside of the orange, being careful not to break the skin. Rinse out with cold water, shake the water out well. Fill $\frac{1}{3}$ full with jelly, colored red with cochineal, set in ice; when this jelly hardens, fill $\frac{2}{3}$ full with orange jelly, let this harden, and fill the last third with jelly colored with coffee, chocolate, or the juice squeezed from spinach leaves. When very hard, cut the oranges with a sharp knife, into quarters, and serve on a bed of green, or cut nearly through and pull the quarters apart, and serve one to each person on a bed of smilax.

ORANGE BASKETS.

With a sharp pointed knife cut a basket with a handle, out of a whole orange. Carefully scoop out the inside, fill the basket with jelly or bavarian cream; when hard, put a little whipped cream on the top, tie a ribbon bow on the handle, and serve on a bed of greens.

FRUIT MOUSSE.

$\frac{1}{2}$ box gelatine. 1 pt. cream.
$\frac{1}{2}$ c. cold water. $\frac{1}{2}$ c. boiling water.
1 pt. fruit juice.

Soak the gelatine in the cold water 1 h. Prepare any kind of fruit juice, orange, apricot, pineapple, or strawberry, and sweeten it to taste; the quantity of sugar will vary with the fruit used. Add the $\frac{1}{2}$ c. of boiling water to the gelatine; when dissolved, add the fruit juice, strain, and set in a pan of ice. Stir occasionally. Whip the cream, and when the juice begins to thicken, stir the cream in lightly, and set in a mold. Pack in ice and salt for 3 h.

CHOCOLATE MOUSSE.

½ box gelatine.
½ c. cold water.
2 squares of W. Baker & Co.'s chocolate.
1 qt. cream.
4 tbsp. sugar.

Soak the gelatine in the cold water 2 h. Whip the cream until you have 1 c. liquid left. Heat this to the boiling point, pour over the gelatine; when dissolved, add the sugar, stir till dissolved, add the chocolate, which has been melted, stir well, strain, and set in a pan of ice. Stir occasionally; when cold, add ½ tsp. vanilla, and when it begins to thicken stir in lightly the whipped cream. Put in a mold. Pack in ice and salt 3 h. Turn out and serve with soft custard.

BAVARIAN CREAM.

¼ box gelatine.
¼ c. cold water.
1 c. cream.
1 c. milk.
Yolks 2 eggs.
¼ c. sugar.
¼ ssp. salt.
½ tsp. vanilla.

Soak the gelatine in cold water 2 h. Whip the cream till you have ¼ c. liquid left; add ½ c. milk to the ½ c. of cream, put on the fire to scald. Beat the yolks, add the sugar and salt, pour the milk over them, return to the fire and cook till thick as custard, stirring all the time. Remove from the fire, add the gelatine, strain, and set in a pan of ice. Stir occasionally, and when it begins to thicken, fold in the whipped cream, set in a mold on the ice.

CHOCOLATE BAVARIAN CREAM.

½ box gelatine.   ½ c. sugar.
½ c. cold milk.   ⅛ ssp. salt.
1 pt. cream.   ½ tsp. vanilla.
1 pt. milk.   Yolks 4 eggs.
2 sq. W. Baker & Co's chocolate.

Soak the gelatine in the ½ c. milk 1 h. Heat the milk in the double boiler, beat the eggs, add the sugar and salt, pour the hot milk over the eggs, return to the double boiler, and cook till like very thick cream; add the chocolate, which has been melted, stir well, strain, and set in a pan of ice. Stir occasionally, and when it begins to thicken, stir in lightly the whipped cream. Set in a mold and serve very cold. Set in ice and salt 3 h.

ORANGE BAVARIAN CREAM.

½ c. cold water.   ¾ c. milk.
½ box gelatine.   1 c. sugar.
1 c. orange juice. Yolks 4 eggs.
3 pts. whipped cream.

If you whip the cream with a whip churn, you will need one pint of liquid cream to make three pints of whipped. Soak the gelatine in the cold water two hours. Scald the milk, beat the yolks, add the sugar, pour over them the scalded milk, stirring all the time; return to the fire and cook till thick as cream, stirring well. Remove from the fire, add the gelatine, stir till dissolved; strain and set aside to cool in a pan of ice; when cool add the orange juice, stir occasionally. Whip the cream, and when the jelly begins to thicken fold in the cream; put in a mold wet with cold water, and set aside to harden.

STRAWBERRY BAVARIAN CREAM.

1 qt. strawberries.	¾ c. milk.
1 pt. cream.	Yolks 4 eggs.
1 c. sugar.	½ box gelatine.

½ c. cold water.

Soak the gelatine in the cold water two hours. Mash the berries and sugar and let stand one hour. Strain the berries, pressing out all but the seeds; scald the milk, beat the eggs, pour the milk over the eggs, stirring all the time; return to the fire and cook till thick as cream, stirring well; remove from the fire, add the gelatine; when dissolved strain and set in a pan of ice, add the juice of the berries and stir occasionally. Whip the cream, and when the jelly begins to thicken, fold it in quickly and lightly. Set it in a mold to harden.

BLANC MANGE.

1 qt. milk.	½ c. sugar.
½ box gelatine.	½ tsp. almond flavoring.

Soak the gelatine in ½ c. cold milk 2 h. Put the milk on to heat and pour over the gelatine, add the sugar; when dissolved strain; when cool add the flavoring and put in a mold, wet in cold water. Serve very cold.

LEMON JELLY.

½ box gelatine.	1 c. sugar.
½ c. cold water.	⅔ c. lemon juice.
1 pt. boiling water.	1 square inch stick cinnamon.

The yellow rind of 1 lemon.

Soak the gelatine in the cold water 2 h. Pour the boiling water over the gelatine, cinnamon and lemon rind, and soak for 5 m.; covered. Add the sugar;

when dissolved add the lemon juice, strain and pour in a mold dipped in cold water.

ORANGE JELLY.

½ box gelatine.   Juice 1 lemon.
½ c. cold water.   1 c. sugar.
1 c. boiling water.   1 pt. orange juice.
Rind of 1 orange.   1 square inch stick cinnamon.

Soak the gelatine in the cold water 2 h. Put the cinnamon and thin rind of the orange in the boiling water, cover and let stand for 5 m. Pour over the gelatine; when dissolved, add the sugar, stir till dissolved; add the lemon and orange juice, strain and set in a mold dipped in cold water.

APPLES IN JELLY.

Prepare the apples as for apples for luncheon. Put one layer in a mold or glass dish. Make the orange jelly, using 1 c. orange juice instead of 2 c. Pour this over the apples and serve very cold, with whipped cream over or around the mold.

CARAMEL.

1 c. gran. sugar.   1 c. boiling water.

Put the sugar in a frying-pan; when it is melted and slightly brown, add the water and simmer ten minutes.

APPLE SNOW.

3 tart apples.   4 tbsp. powd. sugar.   Whites 3 eggs.

Core and quarter the apples and steam till tender and mash through a sieve. When the apples are cold, beat the whites very stiff, add the sugar gradually, then the apple. Pile in a glass dish and decorate with bits of jelly.

PUDDING SAUCES.

LEMON SAUCE.

1 c. hot water. Grated rind and juice of 1 lemon.
½ c. sugar. ½ tbsp. butter.
2 tsp. cornstarch.

Mix the sugar and cornstarch well; pour on the boiling water, stirring all the time. Boil 10 m., add the lemon juice, rind and butter. Serve at once.

FOAMY SAUCE.

½ c. butter. 2 tbsp. fruit juice.
1 c. powdered sugar. White of 1 or 2 eggs.
1 tsp. vanilla. ¼ c. boiling water.

Cream the butter, add the sugar gradually, then the vanilla and fruit juice. When ready to serve add the boiling water, and the egg beaten to a foam.

CREAMY SAUCE.

¼ c. butter. ¼ c. cream.
½ c. powdered sugar. 1 tsp. vanilla.

Cream the butter, add the sugar gradually, then the flavoring and lastly the cream. It will look curdled, but just before serving place the bowl over hot water and stir till smooth.

HARD SAUCE.

½ c. butter. 1 c. powd. sugar.
White 1 egg. ½ tsp. vanilla.

Cream the butter, add the sugar gradually, beat till very light, add the vanilla; add the beaten white last. You may leave out the egg and have a very nice sauce.

PUDDING SAUCES.

CARAMEL SAUCE.

1 c. granulated sugar.   1 c. boiling water.

Put the sugar in a frying-pan, cook till dark brown, add the water and simmer 10 m. Set away to cool.

FRUIT SAUCE.

1 pt. boiling water.   1 pt. canned fruit.
1 c. sugar.   1 tbsp. cornstarch.
⅓ c. cold water.

Moisten the cornstarch in the cold water, stir into the boiling water, add the sugar and boil 10 m. Add the fruit and serve.

LEMON SYRUP (for Waffles.)

1 c. sugar.   1 tsp. butter.
½ c. water.   1 tbsp. lemon juice.

Boil the sugar and water 8 m. Add the butter and lemon juice; when the butter is melted, serve.

CHOCOLATE SAUCE.

1 c. milk.   ½ c. sugar.
¼ tsp. vanilla.   Yolks 2 eggs.
1 sq. W. Baker & Co.'s chocolate.

Scald the milk, add the chocolate, grated, to it; beat the eggs, add the sugar to them; pour the milk over the eggs, return to the fire and cook till thick as cream, stirring all the time. Remove from the fire, strain, and when cold add the flavoring.

ORANGE SAUCE.

½ c. butter.   ¼ c. boiling water.
1 c. powd. sugar.   2 tbsp. orange juice.
1 tsp. vanilla.   ½ tsp. grated rind.
White 1 egg.

Cream the butter, add the sugar gradually, then the vanilla and fruit juice. Just before serving add the boiling water, stir well, add the well-beaten egg, and beat till foamy. Do not beat up the egg until you add it to the sauce, and it must be served the minute the water is added.

HARD SAUCE (with fruit.)

¾ c. butter.
1½ c. powd. sugar.
½ c. gran. sugar.
½ tsp. vanilla.
White of 1 egg.
1 c. berries (strawberries or raspberries).

Cut the berries in halves or quarters, sprinkle with the granulated sugar and let stand for fifteen minutes. Cream the butter, add the powdered sugar gradually, then the vanilla, and the well-beaten egg. Just before serving add the berries.

CUSTARD SAUCE.

2 c. milk.
3 eggs.
3 tbsp. gran. sugar.
1 tsp. vanilla.
½ ssp. salt.

Scald the milk, beat the eggs, salt and sugar together, pour on the scalded milk, return to the fire and cook till thick as cream, stirring all the time. Remove at once from the fire or it will curdle; strain, and when cold add the flavoring.

CAKE.

Cake should always be mixed in an earthen bowl and with a wooden spoon. When baking-powder, or soda, and cream of tartar are used, sift them with the flour. Cream the butter, add the sugar, then the well-beaten yolks, then the flour, with the raising powders sifted with it, alternating with the milk, and lastly, the well-beaten whites. In cakes that have no butter in, such as sponge cakes, the rule is to beat the yolks very light, add the sugar gradually, then the water, and flavoring, and lastly, the well-beaten whites. Do not beat after the whites are added. In sponge cake, where there is no raising powder used, it is the air that you entangle in the eggs that raises the cake, so be very careful not to *stir*, and so break the air bubbles. Fine grained granulated sugar makes the best cake, and the flour should always be perfectly dry. For sponge cake, always dry the flour by the fire, and sift it three times just before using. Choose the dark-shelled eggs if you want a deep-colored cake. Line all large pans with paper, to prevent burning on the bottom. The smaller and thinner the cake, the hotter the oven. In baking loaf cakes, be sure that you can control the fire, so as to have the heat last throughout the baking. Molasses cakes require a cooler oven than others. A loaf, or pound cake, should first rise well before it begins to brown; then begin to brown slightly, and after it is brown all over, shrink from the pan and settle a little. If you move it, or bang the oven door while the walls of the cake are soft, you will make it fall. Open and close the oven door carefully, and slowly, and if it browns too soon, shield it with a piece of brown paper. When a straw comes out clean it is done. Take out of the pan at once, and turn the pan upside down, wipe off and stand the cake on it. Never put it away until cold.

GINGER BREAD.

½ c. molasses. 1 tbsp. butter (softened.)
½ level tbsp. ginger. ¼ c. boiling water.
¼ tsp. salt. 1 c. sifted flour. ½ level tsp. soda.

Put the molasses in a bowl, sift into it the soda, salt, and ginger; add the butter; stir, add the boiling water and flour. Beat well, and bake in shallow pan 20 m.

SOFT MOLASSES COOKIES.

1 c. molasses. 2 tbsp. warm water.
1 level tbsp. ginger. ⅓ c. cottolene (softened.)
1 " tsp. soda. 1 level tsp. salt.
Flour to make a soft dough.

Sift the ginger and salt into the molasses, put the soda into the warm water, and strain into the molasses; add the cottolene, and flour enough to make a dough soft enough to roll out ⅓ of an inch thick. Cut in small rounds, and bake in hot oven.

DOUGHNUTS.

1 pt. flour. ½ ssp. cinnamon.
¼ c. sugar. ¾ c. milk.
½ tsp. salt. 1 egg.
1 tsp. Cleveland's baking- 1 tsp. butter (melted.)
    powder.

Sift the baking-powder, salt, and cinnamon, with the flour; add the sugar, beat the egg, add the milk to the egg, and stir into the flour. Roll out ½ inch thick, cut out, and fry in hot cottolene.

NEW ENGLAND DOUGHNUTS.

1 c. sugar.	2 tsp. melted cottolene.
2 eggs.	½ c. milk.
1 ssp. cinnamon.	½ tsp. salt.
2 tsp. Cleveland's baking-powder.	Flour to make a soft dough.

Beat the eggs very light, add the sugar, beat well, add the cottolene; sift the salt and baking-powder with the flour, add the milk and flour. Roll out and cut out; fry in hot cottolene. Use 1 c. flour to start with.

GINGER SNAPS.

1 c. sugar.	¼ c. cold water.
1 c. molasses.	1 level tbsp. ginger.
1 c. cottolene.	½ " " cinnamon.
3 pts. flour.	1 " tsp. soda.
	1 level tsp. salt.

Cream the cottolene, add the sugar, gradually, then the molasses, salt, and spice. Add the soda, dissolved in the water, and the flour, gradually. Roll out very thin, cut in round cakes, and bake on a greased pan in hot oven.

SOFT MOLASSES GINGERBREAD.

1 c. molasses.	2 tbsp. cottolene.
¼ c. sour milk.	½ tsp. salt (level.)
¾ c. flour. 1 egg.	1 " soda "
1 tsp. cinnamon (level.)	1 tbsp. ginger (level.)

Put the molasses and cottolene on the fire in a

bowl; when warm, add the salt, soda, and spice, sifted through a very fine sieve. Add the sour milk, the egg, well beaten, and the flour. Beat well, bake in a well-greased pan in a hot oven.

LUNCH CAKE.

1 tbsp. butter. $1\frac{1}{2}$ c. flour.
1 scant c. sugar. $\frac{3}{4}$ c. milk (scant.)
1 egg. $\frac{3}{4}$ c. currants.
1 tsp. Cleveland's baking-powder.

Cream the butter, add the sugar, gradually, add the well-beaten egg; sift the flour and the baking-powder, add the flour and the milk, gradually, lastly, the currants. Bake in a loaf pan, lined with greased paper, about 40 m.

CURRANT LUNCH CAKES.

1 tbsp. cottolene. $1\frac{1}{2}$ c. flour.
1 c. sugar. $\frac{3}{4}$ c. milk.
1 egg. $\frac{3}{4}$ c. currants.
1 ssp. cloves. $\frac{1}{2}$ tsp. cinnamon.
1 tsp. Cleveland's baking-powder.

Cream the cottolene, add the sugar, gradually, then the well-beaten eggs; sift the spices and baking-powder with the flour, add the milk and flour gradually, and lastly, the currants. Bake in small pans about 15 m.

CURRANT AND RAISIN LUNCH CAKE.

2 tbsp. cottolene. $1\frac{1}{2}$ c. flour.
2 eggs. $\frac{1}{4}$ c. milk.
1 c. sugar. $\frac{1}{2}$ c. raisins.
2 tsp. Cleveland's baking-powder. $\frac{1}{2}$ c. currants.

Cream the cottolene, add the sugar, gradually, add the well-beaten eggs; sift the baking-powder with the flour, add it, alternating with the milk. Give a good beating, then add the raisins, which have been stoned and cut into halves, and the currants, which have been washed and dried. Bake in small pans, in a hot oven, 15 to 20 minutes.

CUP CAKE.

1 c. butter. 4 eggs.
2 c. sugar. 1 c. milk.
3 c. flour. 1 tsp. flavoring.
2 tsp. Cleveland's baking-powder.

Cream the butter, add the sugar, then the well-beaten yolks; sift the baking-powder with the flour, add the flour and milk, alternating, then the flavoring, and lastly, the whites, beaten stiff. Do not beat or stir much after adding the whites.

LAYER CAKE.

½ c. butter. 4 eggs.
2 c. sugar. 1 c. milk.
3 c. flour. 2 tsp. Cleveland's baking-powder.

Cream the butter, add the sugar, gradually; beat the eggs, yolks and whites together; add to the butter and sugar; sift the baking-powder with the flour, and add with the milk. Spread with a knife on buttered tins, and bake in a quick oven about 15 m.

NUT CAKE.

Add to the layer cake 1½ c. chopped nuts and bake in a loaf.

NUT LAYER CAKE.

Bake the layers as by the recipe for layer cake. Spread the layers with the boiled icing, sprinkle with chopped nuts, put on another layer, etc. Spread the top with icing, and decorate with whole, or half nuts.

ORANGE LAYER CAKE.

Make the layers as by recipe for layer cake.

FILLING.

Juice and rind of 1 orange. 1 egg.
1 scant c. milk. 2 tbsp. gran. sugar.
2 tsp. cornstarch.

Mix the cornstarch with a little cold milk. Heat the remainder of the milk to boiling, add the cornstarch, cook 5 m., stirring well, add the well-beaten egg and the sugar, and lastly the orange.

COCOANUT CAKE.—LAYER.

Make the layers as by recipe for layer cake. Spread with boiled icing, in which you have put 1 tsp. lemon juice; sprinkle with fresh, grated cocoanut. Repeat until all the layers are used, and cover the top and sides with icing, and sprinkle with cocoanut.

CHOCOLATE LAYER CAKE.

Make the layers as by recipe for layer cake. Add to the boiled icing, when hot, 2 squares of W. Baker & Co.'s chocolate, melted, and $\frac{1}{4}$ tsp. vanilla. Spread between the layers and on the top.

RAISIN LAYER CAKE.

Spread between the layers the boiled icing to which you have added 1 c. chopped raisins and $\frac{1}{4}$ tsp. vanilla. Reserve a little icing plain, for the top, and decorate with raisins pressed flat and round.

RAISIN LAYER CAKE NO. 2.

$\frac{3}{4}$ c. cottolene. 1 c. milk.
2 c. sugar. 3 c. sifted flour.
3 eggs. 1 c. raisins.
2 tsp. Cleveland's baking-powder.

Cream the cottolene, add the sugar gradually, then the yolks, well beaten. Sift the baking-powder with the flour, add it to the batter, alternating with the milk. Beat the whites stiff, add them last. Divide the mixture in half; add to one half the raisins, which have been stoned and cut in half. Fill two layer cake pans with the plain dough, and two with the raisin dough. Bake, spread with cream filling, putting the raisin cake between the plain.

CREAM FILLING.

1½ c. milk.	2 eggs.
1 tbsp. cornstarch.	¼ c. sugar.
1 tsp. butter.	½ ssp. salt.

½ tsp. vanilla flavoring.

Mix the cornstarch with a little cold milk, add the salt; scald the rest of the milk, add the cornstarch; cook five minutes, stirring constantly. Add the sugar and butter, and when cold add the flavoring. Put between the layers and cover with an icing, made of the white of an egg beaten to a stiff froth, and one tablespoonful of powdered sugar.

MOLASSES FRUIT CAKE.

1 c. butter.	Yolks 3 eggs.
1¼ c. brown sugar.	Whites 2 eggs.
½ c. currants.	½ c. milk.
½ lb. stoned raisins.	4 c. flour.
1 ssp. salt.	3 tsp. mixed spices.
½ c. molasses.	½ tsp. soda.

Cream the butter, add the sugar, add the yolks of

the eggs and the molasses, beat well. Sift the baking-powder and spices with the flour, add the flour, alternating with the milk, then the whites, beaten stiff. Then the fruit. Bake 1½ hours if in a loaf, 30 m. if in small pans.

SPONGE CAKE.

3 eggs.	2 c. sifted flour.
1½ c. gran. sugar.	1 tsp. lemon extract.
½ c. cold water.	2 tsp. Cleveland's baking-
½ ssp. salt.	powder.

Sift the flour, salt and baking-powder three times. Separate the eggs. Beat the yolks with a dover beater 2 m. Add the sugar, beating 2 m.; add the water and the lemon extract. Add the flour, beating 2 m. Beat the whites of the eggs 2 m. Fold them in, do not beat or stir, put into a loaf pan lined with greased paper, and bake about 30 m.

SPONGE CAKE NO. 2.

12 eggs.	3 c. sifted flour.
1 lemon, juice and rind.	3 c. sugar.

Dry the flour before the fire for several hours. Just before using, sift it three times. Separate the eggs, beat the yolks for 2 m., add the sugar, beat 2 m., add the lemon; beat the whites 2 m., cut them in lightly, and fold the flour in carefully. Do not stir or beat after the whites are added. Bake about 30 m.

LADY CAKE.

2 c. sugar.	½ c. butter.
2½ c. sifted flour.	¾ c. milk.
½ tsp. almond flavoring.	Whites 8 eggs.
1½ tsp. Cleveland's baking-powder.	

Cream the butter, add the sugar; sift the baking-powder with the flour, add it alternately with the milk, add the flavoring; lastly, fold in lightly the whites. Bake in a loaf for about 40 m.

BOILED ICING.

2 c. sugar.   Whites of 2 eggs.
6 tbsp. water, hot.

Boil the water and sugar till the syrup ropes when dropped in cold water. Do not stir after the sugar is melted. Pour slowly over the well-beaten whites, beating all the time, and beat till nearly cold.

ORNAMENTAL FROSTING.

Beat the whites of two eggs stiff, add gradually 2 tbsp. powd. sugar, beat well; make a cornucopia of white paper, put the frosting in, cut a small hole in the end, and squeeze the frosting through in any design you please.

STRAWBERRY SHORTCAKE.

4 c. flour.   2 tbsp. butter.
1 tsp. salt.   1 qt. berries.
$1\frac{3}{4}$ c. milk.   1 pt. cream.
2 tsp. Cleveland's baking-powder.

Sift the salt, baking-powder and flour; rub in the butter, add sufficient milk to make a soft dough. Roll out one and one-half inches thick, and put in a well-greased pan, bake in a hot oven twenty minutes. Stem the berries, cut into quarters if large, halves if small, reserving one-third handsome ones for the top. Sprinkle the berries with sugar. When the cake is done, remove from the pan, split in half and spread lightly with butter. Put the berries between the layers and the large ones on top. Dust a little powdered sugar over the top, and pile the whipped cream around the base.

Peach and raspberry shortcake are prepared the same, and are very delicious.

RASPBERRY TRIFLE.

1 qt. raspberries.	2 eggs.
1½ c. milk.	2 tbsp. gran. sugar.
¼ tsp. lemon extract.	2 " powd. "

Stale sponge cake.

Scald the milk, beat the yolks of the eggs, add the gran. sugar; beat, and pour the milk on the eggs. Return to the fire, cook until thick as cream, stirring all the time; strain, and set aside to cool. When cold add the flavoring. Cover a dish with a thin layer of cake, then a layer of raspberries, pour over a little custard. Repeat, and let the top be raspberries, piled up in a pyramid. Beat the whites of the eggs stiff, add the powd. sugar and heap around the base. Serve very cold.

CHANTILLY BASKET.

1 c. sugar.   1 ssp. cream of tartar.
½ c. boiling water.

Boil all together without stirring, until it is brittle when dropped from the end of a fork into cold water. Have stale maccaroons right at your hand, and a greased plate. Set the syrup in a pan of hot water, dip each maccaroon into the syrup, wetting only the edges; stick together and form a basket on the greased plate.

PASTRY AND PIES.

PASTRY.

To make light, flaky pastry, have everything very cold and the oven hot. Use only the best of flour and shortening. Handle as little as possible, chopping in and mixing with a knife. If the pastry gets at all soft, lay aside in a napkin on the ice and have it cold when it goes into the oven. Never grease a pie plate before putting on the paste.

PASTRY FOR ONE PIE.

1 c. flour.   ¼ c. butter.
¼ c. lard.   Ice water to make stiff dough.
1 ssp. salt.   1 ssp. Cleveland's baking powder.

Sift the salt and baking powder with the flour, chop in the lard, mix quite stiff with cold water. Roll out, put the butter on the paste in small pieces, sprinkle with a little flour, fold over and roll out. Repeat three times. Roll out thin and use for one pie.

PUFF PASTE.

1 lb. butter.   ½ tsp. sugar.
1 lb. flour.   ½ tsp. salt.
White 1 egg.   1 c. ice water, more or less.

Sift the flour, salt and sugar on to a marble slab. Make a hole in the centre and put butter, the size of an egg, and the white of the egg. The butter is much better if it has been washed before using, by working with the hands under ice water until smooth and elastic, and then laying on the ice to harden; but it can be used without washing. Work the flour, butter and white of egg, adding a little water at a time until all the flour is used. Knead as you would bread for a few minutes, roll out very thin, lay the remainder of the butter on half, sprinkle with a little flour, fold over and roll out. Roll out and fold over eight times, and when it becomes at all soft lay in a damp napkin on the ice till hard. Let it stand on the ice several hours before baking, over night is the best. When put into the oven the pastry should be icy cold, and the oven should be very hot. Put the pastry in a part of the oven where there may be a good heat underneath, that it may rise before browning; should it begin to brown reduce the heat at once. Only practice can possibly teach one just the heat and how to regulate it.

APPLE PIE.

Never grease a pie plate before putting the paste in. Greenings make the best cooking apples, and the quantity of sugar used must be according to the tartness of the apples. Line a plate with plain paste, core, pare and quarter the apples, put a layer of the quarters on the paste, sprinkle with sugar mixed with a little cinnamon, and a very little grated lemon rind. Repeat until the apples are quite high. Roll the pastry for the top crust very thin, fold in half, cut several small gashes in the centre, wet the rim of the lower crust and lay the upper crust on, filling it in, that it may not draw away the paste from the pan. Press the edges together, put a narrow strip of pastry around the edge and bake in a hot oven 30 to 40 m.

CHERRY PIE.

Prepare the same as apple pie, filling the centre with stoned cherries, using sugar only.

HUCKLEBERRY PIE.

Prepare the same as apple pie, using sugar only, first washing the huckleberries and drying well. Press the edges well together that the juice may not run out.

LEMON MERINGUE PIE.

Line a plate with paste, put two extra strips around the edge, wetting the edge slightly with ice water before putting on each rim, and fill with the following mixture. Bake 30 m., remove from the oven, and when the pie is cool, cover with the meringue; place in a cool, oven 15 m.

FILLING.

2 eggs. 4 tbsp. powd. sugar.
4 tbsp. gran. sugar. 1 scant c. milk.
1 tsp. cornstarch. Juice and rind of 1 lemon.

Mix the cornstarch with a little of the milk, scald the rest and add the cornstarch, stirring well, boil 1 m.; cool, add the yolks of the eggs, the sugar and the lemon, beat well. When cold fill the pie with this and bake 30 m. Remove from the oven and cover with a meringue made by beating the whites stiff, adding the powd. sugar gradually; pile this on the top and place in a cool oven 15 m.

PUMPKIN PIE.

Pare the pumpkin and stew in just enough water to cover. Mash through a sieve and to 1 qt. of pumpkin add 3 eggs, 1 tsp. ground mace, 1 tsp. cinnamon, 1 tsp. ginger. Mix all together and add sugar and salt to taste. Thin it with a little milk, and bake in a deep pie plate, lined with good plain paste, about 30 m.

PLAIN MINCE PIES.

1 c. meat.	½ c. raisins.
2 c. apples.	½ c. currants.
1 level tsp. salt.	½ c. water.
" " cinnamon.	⅓ c. molasses.
1 " " allspice.	1½ c. brown sugar.

Juice and grated rind of 2 lemons.

Chop small pieces of tender beef very fine. Chop the apples and stoned raisins fine. Boil the water, sugar, spice and raisins 10 m., add the other ingredients and cook till the apples are soft. When cool make into pies.

TARTS OR PATTIES.

Roll out puff paste ¾ inch thick. Cut out rounds with a tin cutter. Lay one on a sheet of paper on a tin pan. Cut smaller rounds out of three others and put the rings on top of the first round, being careful to rub only the top with white of egg. Do not put any egg on the top round, and be careful not to let the egg run down on the sides, or it will prevent the paste from rising. Bake on the papers in a hot oven. For patties you may put rounds of stale bread in the centre to prevent rising; remove when done. Bake enough small rounds to make covers for the cases.

LEMON MERINGUE TARTS.

Line small patty pans with plain paste, put two narrow strips of pastry around each pan, and proceed as for lemon meringue pie.

CRANBERRY TARTS.

Line small patty pans with plain crust, putting two strips of pastry round the edge; fill with uncooked rice and bake till the pastry is done. Remove the rice and fill with stewed cranberries.

PEACH TARTLETS A LA ITALIAN.

Line out small patty pans with any kind of good paste, put a piece of bread or a little uncooked rice in, and bake. When done, remove the rice and let cool. When cold, place in the centre of each tartlet a half of a preserved peach, hollow side uppermost; fill this hollow with whipped cream, piled high; surround this with a delicate pink border made of the white of one egg, beaten stiff; then add one tablespoonful of powdered sugar and a few drops of cochineal. Serve on a fancy paper. You may use apricots in place of peaches, if you desire.

BAKED APPLE DUMPLINGS.

1 qt. flour. 2 tbsp. lard.
1 ssp. salt. 1 " beef drippings.
1 pt. milk. 2 tsp. Cleveland's baking-powder.

Sift the baking-powder, salt and flour, and chop in the lard and dripping. Add enough milk to make a soft paste, roll out half an inch thick, cut into squares. Core and pare tart, juicy apples, and put one in the centre of the paste, sprinkle with a little sugar mixed with a little cinnamon, bring the corners of the square together, pinch them and lay on a buttered baking tin, with the joined edges downward. Bake in a hot oven about forty minutes. When done, brush over with beaten egg, set in the oven till dry. Serve with hard or creamy sauce.

ICE CREAMS AND SHERBETS.

FREEZING.

One of the necessary articles that ought to be found in every kitchen, is a good ice cream freezer, for the days of hot and heavy puddings, and more indigestible pastry, are fast being superseded by the delicious and wholesome dainties found in many homes, even of the laboring classes. The most incompetent cook can, without fail, prepare many a surprise in the way of a dessert, that would do credit to a caterer, and for far less cost than the material formerly used, with such distressing results. In sickness a freezer is indispensible, for in a few moments, before the desire of the patient can change, you have something at hand that is refreshing and harmless. After using many of the freezers in the market, I can heartily recommend the "White Mountain" as far the best in every way; economical, quick to freeze, and the triple action of the beater producing a far more delicate sherbet, and a much smoother, finer grained cream.

The principal points to be remembered in freezing are, that the proper proportions of ice and salt are used, the ice crushed fine, and the beater turned quickly, if a smooth texture is desired.

DIRECTIONS FOR FREEZING.

See that the can is perfectly clean, all the parts adjusted properly, the bearings and socket in the tub well oiled, and the crank turn easily, before putting in the cream. Have the material to be frozen very cold before putting into the freezer. Turn in the cream, adjust the cover, and fasten the latch. Throw around the can three small plates of ice, chopped as fine as the rock salt, then one plate of rock salt (not coarse salt, but rock salt used for freezing), three more of ice, and one of salt, and so on, until it reaches to the top of the can. Pack down carefully with the handle of a wooden spoon, turning the crank occasionally, to see that all is right. Do not put large pieces of ice in, as they dent the freezer, and the cream will not freeze as quick as with finely crushed ice. Keep the plug in, but watch carefully, that the water does not rise to the top of the can, or it will salt the cream. Be careful not to let the ice and salt touch the working of the freezer above the can. It is the temperature of the water, which is much lower than the temperature of ice, that draws out the heat from the contents of the can and freezes the liquid, so do not draw off the entire water, unless to keep for several hours. Turn the crank slowly for 5 m., then as quick as you can, and do not leave it until done. Add all fruit and whipped cream when partly frozen. When the cream is frozen, remove the dasher, scrape the sides of the can, stir well, cover. Cover the hole made by the dasher with a small tin patty pan, or cover of a baking powder box, drain off the water, pack with ice and salt, cover with piece of carpet, wet in salt and water, plug up the hole, and set away to ripen for two or three hours.

TO MOLD CREAM.

Dip the mold in cold water. When the cream is

frozen quite stiff, pack in the mold, filling every corner. Have the cover fit tightly and *over* the can. Fill the crack of the opening with melted suet, to keep out the water. Pack in ice and salt, and when ready to serve, dip quickly in lukewarm water ; wipe off, remove the cover, and turn out on a platter.

VANILLA ICE CREAM.

1¼ c. gran. sugar.	2 c. cream.
Yolks 3 eggs. 1 tbsp. vanilla.	2 c. milk.

Scald the milk in a double boiler; beat the eggs, add ½ c. sugar; pour the milk on the eggs, stirring well; return to the double boiler and cook until thick as cream, stirring all the time. Remove from the fire, add the rest of the sugar; when cold, add the flavoring, cream, and freeze.

CHOCOLATE ICE CREAM.

Make the same as the vanilla ice cream ; while hot, add two squares of W. Baker & Co.'s chocolate, and use 1 tsp. of vanilla, instead of 1 tbsp.

LEMON ICE CREAM.

Make the same as vanilla ice cream, and use lemon flavoring, instead of vanilla.

BANANA ICE CREAM.

Make the same as vanilla ice cream, using no vanilla, and when half frozen add two good sized red bananas, which have been cut into small pieces. Use no flavoring, but the banana.

COFFEE ICE CREAM.

1 pt. milk.	Yolks 4 eggs.
1 pt. cream.	¼ c. strong black coffee.
	1 c. sugar.

Scald the milk in a double boiler. Beat the yolks, add ⅓ the sugar, pour the milk on the eggs, stirring well; return to the fire, cook till like thick cream; remove from the fire, add the rest of the sugar. When cold, add the coffee, and cream and freeze.

STRAWBERRY ICE CREAM.

Make the same as vanilla ice cream, leaving out the vanilla, and, when partly frozen, add 1 pt. of strawberries, which have been cut fine, and sugared to taste. Turn the crank rapidly for 10 m., after adding the fruit.

PEACH ICE CREAM.

1 qt. peaches.   2 c. sugar.
1 qt. milk.   4 eggs (yolks).

Pare, and cut up the peaches, which should be perfectly ripe, into very small pieces, add one cup of sugar to them, and let them stand for three or four hours. Scald the milk, beat the eggs and half a cup of sugar, pour the scalded milk over the eggs, return to the fire, and cook till thick as cream, stirring all the time. Remove from the fire, add the remaining half cup of sugar; when dissolved, strain, and set aside to cool. When cold, add the peaches, and freeze. Should the peaches be tart, they may need a little more sugar.

APRICOT ICE CREAM.

Prepare the same as peach ice cream.

BISQUE ICE CREAM.

1 qt. milk.   1 c. sugar.
4 eggs (yolks).   ½ lb. stale maccaroons.
4 kisses.   1 tsp. vanilla.
    1 tsp. caramel.

Scald the milk, beat the eggs, add half the sugar, pour the milk on to the eggs, stirring well; return to the fire, and cook till like cream, stirring all the time. Remove from the fire, strain, and when cold, add the caramel and vanilla. Pound and roll the maccaroons, and kisses, and when the cream is partly frozen, add them; turn the crank well after adding them, until the cream is hard enough to set away and freeze.

PHILADELPHIA ICE CREAM.

1 qt. cream.   1 c. sugar.   1 tbsp. vanilla.

Whip the cream until you have 1 qt. froth. Add the sugar and flavoring to the liquid left, and freeze it. When frozen, fold in lightly the whipped cream, and set aside for 2 h.

CARAMEL ICE CREAM.

Melt 1 c. sugar till brown, add 4 tbsp. hot milk, boil 5 m., set away to cool. Put in a double boiler 1 pt. milk. Mix to a smooth paste $\frac{1}{3}$ c. flour, add 1 c. sugar, and 2 eggs. Pour the boiling milk on this, return to the fire, and boil 20 m. Let cool, add the milk and sugar first cooked together, 1 qt. cream, and freeze.

DELMONICO ICE CREAM.

1 qt. cream.   1 c. sugar.
Yolks 6 eggs. $\frac{1}{2}$ tbsp. vanilla.

Scald the cream, beat the eggs, add half the sugar, pour the cream over the eggs, return to the fire, and cook till thick as cream, stirring all the time; remove from the fire, add the rest of the sugar; when dissolved, strain, and when cool, add the vanilla, and freeze.

TUTTI FRUTTI.

Prepare the Delmonico ice cream; when cold, add 1 pt. more of cold cream, and use 1 tbsp. of vanilla instead of ½ tbsp. Freeze, and when almost hard add the following, cut up into small pieces:

½ c. candied pineapple.   ½ c. candied cherries.
¼ c.   "   rhubarb.   ½ c.   "   apricots.

You may add the fruit to the plain vanilla cream, and you can use any kind or quantity of fruit you desire. After the fruit is added, turn the crank quickly for 5 m.

FROZEN CUSTARD.

1 c. sugar.   Yolks 6 eggs.
1 qt. milk.   ½ ssp. salt.
             ½ tbsp. flavoring.

Scald the milk, beat the eggs, add ½ c. sugar and the salt; pour the milk over the eggs, return to the fire, cook till thick as cream, stirring all the time. Remove from the fire, add the rest of the sugar, and when cold add the flavoring and freeze.

SHERBETS.

Sherbets, or ices, are made by freezing the juice of fruit, mixed with sugar and water. Sometimes a tablespoonful of gelatine is added to give the sherbet a firmer consistency. They take much longer to freeze, and need to be beaten very much, in order to produce a creamy appearance.

ORANGE SHERBET.

1 tbsp. gelatine.   1 c. hot water.
1 pt. orange juice.   1½ c. cold water.
1½ c. sugar. ·   1 lemon.

Soak the gelatine in ½ c. cold water 1 h. Pour the boiling water over it; when dissolved, add the sugar, stir till dissolved, add the orange juice, lemon juice, and the remaining 1 c. cold water. Strain and freeze.

LEMON SHERBET.

Prepare the same as orange sherbet, using 1 c. lemon juice and 2 c. sugar.

STRAWBERRY SHERBET.

1 pt. preserved fruit.	1 pt. cold water.
½ c. cold water.	1 tbsp. gelatine.
1 c. sugar.	2 lemons.
½ c. boiling water.	

Soak the gelatine in the ½ c. cold water 2 h. Add the ½ c. boiling water; when dissolved, add the sugar and the lemon juice. Pour the 1 pt. cold water onto the preserves, and mash all but the seeds through a sieve. Add this to the sugar and water; when dissolved, strain all and freeze.

RASPBERRY SHERBET.

Prepare the same as for strawberry sherbet.

PINEAPPLE ICE.

Pare and remove all the eyes. Grate the pineapple, and to 1 pt. of grated fruit add 1 pt. sugar, 1 pt. water, and use 1 tbsp. gelatine as directed in strawberry sherbet.

LEMON GINGER SHERBET

4 lemons.	1 pt. sugar.
¼ lb. candied ginger.	1 qt. water.
1 tbsp. gelatine.	2 lemons.

Soak the gelatine in ¼ c. cold water 2 h. Pare off the thin yellow rind of the lemons and cut the ginger into small pieces. Heat 2 c. of the 1 qt. of water to boiling, pour over the ginger and lemon peel; steep, closely covered, 10 m., add the gelatine, sugar; when dissolved strain, add the remainder of the water and freeze. Use 1 qt. of water in all.

FROZEN APRICOTS.

½ can apricots.   1 c. sugar.
2 c. water.   1 c. whipped cream.

Put the apricots and sugar in a bowl. Cut up with a knife and fork into small pieces; add the water, and when the sugar is dissolved, freeze. When partly frozen remove the dasher and fold in the cream. They are delicious without the cream. Prepare frozen peaches, strawberries and other fruits the same way.

CAFÉ PARFAIT.

2 c. cream.   1 c. sugar.
½ c. strong coffee.

Put all together in a bowl, set in ice, whip and take the froth off on to sieve set in a bowl. Let it drain 10 m., then put lightly into a freezer packed in ice and salt. Cover tight and freeze 3 h.

GRAPE SHERBET.

1 pt. water.   1 c. grape juice.
1 c. sugar.

Mix; when the sugar is dissolved, freeze. You may take one cup of grape preserves and boil with the sugar and water for five minutes; strain it, and when cold, freeze.

FRUIT.

As soon as fruit comes from the market it should be looked over thoroughly and put at once near the ice or in as cool a place as you have. To be delicious, it must be ripe, fresh and cold. Apples, bananas, pears and peaches should be wiped off. Grapes should be rinsed in cold water, drained on a sieve, and cut into small bunches, unless you need the bunches large for decorating. Grapes or cherries look very pretty served in small clusters in a deep glass dish of chipped ice. Oranges may be served whole or cut in half, crosswise. Melons should lie on the ice at least 10 h. before serving, and you may serve the small ones, cut in half and chipped ice in the middle; but this takes away from the delicate flavor. Blackberries, huckleberries and currants should be washed; strawberries, if sandy, may be washed carefully; never wash raspberries, but pick over very gently, seeing that there are no little insects in them. Serve sugar and cream with the fruit, but never put it on it.

BAKED APPLES.

Wipe the apples, remove the core, put on a baking-dish and into each apple put 1 tsp. sugar and 1 tbsp. water. Bake in a hot oven, turning often that they may cook evenly. When done put on a dish carefully and pour a little juice into each apple

APPLE SAUCE.

Have a granite pan $\frac{3}{4}$ full of boiling water. Cut

one apple into quarters, core and pare it, cut the quarters into three slices, and drop at once into the boiling water. Work very quickly until you have three apples done, cover the saucepan and boil about 5 m., until the apples are soft; skim out, drain against the side of the pan, and press immediately through a wire sieve. Put more apples in to boil and continue till all are used. Sweeten to taste. Unless you work quickly, the apple sauce will be dark-colored. Wash the sieve as soon as done thoroughly, as the acid of the apple acts on the wire and produces a poison if left there. Hair sieves are best.

ATALANTA APPLES.

3 apples. 1 inch stick cinnamon.
2 c. sugar. 6 rounds of thin bread.
2 c. boiling water. A little currant jelly.
1 slice of lemon peel.

Boil the sugar, water, lemon and cinnamon 10 m. Halve, core and pare the apples. Cook as many as will float in the boiling syrup, till you can pass a straw through them. Drain from the syrup and dry in the oven a few minutes, and sprinkle with a very little powdered sugar. When all the apples are cooked, dip the rounds of bread quickly in the syrup, lay on a flat dish, spread with jelly and put a piece of apple on each round of bread. Boil the syrup a few minutes more, pour around the apples and set aside to cool. Put a bit of jelly on each apple and serve with whipped cream.

APPLES FOR LUNCHEON.

1 c. sugar. 1 inch stick cinnamon.
1 c. water. 1 slice lemon.

Put all on the fire and boil 10 m. Cut the apple in quarters, pare, core and cook in the boiling syrup till a straw will pass through them. Drain carefully and lay on a flat dish. When all are done strain the syrup and serve over or with the apples.

STEWED PRUNES.

½ lb. prunes. 2 tbsp. sugar.
1 slice lemon. 1 inch stick cinnamon.

Soak the prunes 1 h. in cold water. Pour off the water and cover with boiling water; stew till tender, about ½ h., add the sugar, lemon and cinnamon. Stew uncovered 15 m.

CRANBERRIES.

2 c. cranberries. 1 c. sugar. ⅓ c. cold water.

Wash the cranberries, drain well, put them in a granite pan, put the sugar on top, cover, and when they come to a boil, boil 10 m. Keep them closely covered all the time, and do not stir. Turn out on a dish, and when they cool, they will be like candied cherries.

STEWED FRUIT.

1 c. cold water. 1 c. sugar.

Put on the fire and boil for 10 m., then add the fruit, and simmer till tender. You may add one or two cloves, and a little stick of cinnamon, for pears and peaches, or a slice of lemon, or orange peel, but use no flavoring for berries of any kind, and use ½ c. water when stewing berries.

FRUIT MERINGUE.

Peel and cut up oranges carefully, removing and cutting out the hard centre part, also the white skin under yellow rind. Put a layer of oranges on a glass dish, sprinkle with powdered sugar, then a layer of sliced banana, sprinkle with sugar, squeeze a little lemon juice over the banana, then sprinkle grated cocoanut over. You may continue till all is used, and cover the top with cocoanut, or you may make it without the cocoanut, and cover the whole with a meringue made of the whites of 2 eggs, beaten stiff, and 2 tbsp. powd. sugar, added gradually.

FRUIT BASKETS.

With a sharp pointed knife cut baskets with handles out of whole oranges. Scoop out the oranges, wash out and dry the baskets, and fill with little cubes of banana, grapes, seeded, and cut in halves or quarters, pieces of peach, orange, or any fruit you desire. As you fill it, sprinkle a little powdered sugar on the fruit, and cover the fruit with grated cocoanut, or whipped cream. Tie a bow of ribbon on the handle and serve on a bed of greens. The fruit should be very cold.

BERRY CASES.

1 qt. berries. 1 large sponge cake.
2 c. cream. ¼ c. sugar.

Scoop out the inside of the cake, leaving the walls and bottom one inch thick. Put the cake on the dish it is to be served on; just before serving pour a little cream on the bottom of the cake. Add the sugar to the cream and whip. Fill the opening made in the cake with berries, piled up in the centre; surround the base with whipped cream, and pile whipped cream around the top edge of the cake, resting against the berries and reaching half way up the berries. Serve at once.

RASPBERRY SNOW.

2 c. red raspberries.   ½ c. cold water.
Whites 4 eggs.   1 c. boiling water.
½ box gelatine.   2 c. whipped cream.
            1 c. gran. sugar.

Soak the gelatine in the cold water 2 h. Pour the boiling water over it, add the sugar when dissolved, strain and set in pan of ice. Stir occasionally, and when it begins to thicken, add the beaten whites and whip with a wire spoon till quite stiff; add the berries carefully and put in a mold. Serve with whipped cream around the base and a few berries dotted over the top.

GRATED PINEAPPLES.

Pare the pineapple and remove all the eyes. Grate all but the tough part in the centre, sprinkle with a little sugar, add a little chipped ice. This is very refreshing. It may be frozen by making it a little sweeter, and adding a cup of cold water to every two cups of pineapple.

BEVERAGES.

Have the beverages to be served hot, very hot, and the ones to be served cold, very cold. When water is used to make them it must be freshly boiled, and not stand in the kettle all day or all night. The water, as it boils, loses its gases, and becomes flat and tasteless, and so ruins the flavor of the best tea or coffee.

COFFEE (boiled.)

1 c. ground coffee.   5 c. boiling water.
1 c. cold coffee, or ½ c. cold water.
2 egg shells.

Grind the coffee just before using, mix it with the egg shells and cold water, or coffee. Pour on the boiling water and cover closely, boil 5 m.; draw to one side to settle. In 5 m. add ½ c. cold water, pour a little out to clear the spout, return to the pot and serve. After the meal, drain off the coffee left, and set aside for the cold coffee to use the next time. *Do not keep it in the coffee pot*, but wash the pot out with clear water; never put the dishcloth into it; clean and dry it, and leave partly uncovered till needed again. Rinse out before using with clear, cold water. One-third Mocha and two-thirds Java are the best combination.

FILTERED COFFEE.

Allow 1 tbsp. finely ground coffee to 1 c. water. Put the coffee in the pot, pour the water, which must be freshly boiled, and boiling, not simmering, over the coffee; as it drains through the biggin, fill the top again until all the water required is used. Serve immediately, and be careful that the pot does not stand where it will boil.

CAFE NOIR.

May be made by either recipe, filtered coffee or boiled coffee, using 3 tbsp. coffee to 1 c. water, and if boiled use four egg shells, or the white of one egg mixed with the coffee and cold water.

TEA.

Have the water freshly boiled. Scald the tea pot. Put the tea in the pot, allowing 1 tsp. tea to 1 c. water; pour the boiling water on and steep 5 m. where it will not boil. Serve at once. It is best made in an earthen pot and should never be boiled, as it draws out the tannin and acts as a medicine.

CHOCOLATE.

1 tbsp. sugar.	2 c. scalded milk.
1 square W. Baker & Co.'s chocolate.	$\frac{1}{2}$ tsp. vanilla extract.

Cut the chocolate in small pieces and put it with the sugar and $\frac{1}{4}$ c. milk into a saucepan. Stir over the fire till smooth and glossy. Add the remainder of the milk gradually, and serve at once. If desired richer, use double the quantity of chocolate.

COCOA.

2 tbsp. sugar.   2 c. boiling water.   2 c. milk.
2 tbsp. W. Baker & Co.'s Breakfast Cocoa.

Scald the milk; pour the boiling water gradually over the cocoa and sugar, stirring well all the time, and boil 5 m. Add the scalded milk, strain and serve. A very little whipped cream beaten in at the last improves it.

LEMONADE.

1 lemon.   1 c. boiling water.   1 tbsp. sugar.

Remove the yellow peel by paring very thin, steep in the boiling water 10 m.; cover, strain, add the sugar, and when cold add the lemon juice.

ORANGEADE.

Prepare the same as for lemonade.

SUNDRIES.

BREAD CRUMBS.

Not one crumb of bread should be wasted. The stale slices ought to be toasted and used as a plate of hot toast, or as the foundation of warmed up meat, fish or vegetables, and if not enough to use in that way, small points of toast may be made to decorate with. The soft, white crumbs should be large, and used to cover all dishes made with white sauce, as they make a more delicious combination than the fine, sifted crumbs. The sifted crumbs should have the pieces thoroughly dried, either in a cool oven, or they may be tied up in a paper bag and hung near the fire. Roll them on an old board, as it will spoil a bread board; sift through a fine sieve and put away in covered jar. No burnt or very dark-colored crusts should be used, and the proportion of half crust and half inside makes the most tempting brown when properly fried. They will keep for months, but should always be seasoned before using by shaking a little salt and pepper over them. After using them, sift what is left and save for future use.

BUTTERED BREAD CRUMBS.

1 c. crumbs. $\frac{1}{2}$ tbsp. butter.

Melt the butter and pour slowly over the crumbs, tossing the crumbs lightly with a fork.

CRACKER CRUMBS.

Save any bits of broken crackers, lay in a cool oven till crisp; roll them and sift through a fine sieve.

BREAD SAUTÉD.

1 egg.   1 c. milk.   1 ssp. salt.   1 tbsp. sugar.

Beat the egg in a shallow dish, add the salt, sugar and milk; beat thoroughly and dip stale slices of bread in; when soft, drain and fry in a little hot cottolene, turning over to brown the under side. Sprinkle with a little powdered sugar and serve at once.

TOASTED CRACKERS.

Lay the crackers on a shallow pan and put in a moderate oven till thoroughly heated through. Remove from the oven, spread with a very little butter, return to the oven and bake till a delicate brown.

CRACKERS AND CHEESE.

1 tbsp. grated cheese. $\frac{1}{4}$ ssp. pepper. $\frac{1}{4}$ ssp. salt.

Prepare the toasted crackers, mix the salt, pepper and cheese; spread the crackers, return to the oven, bake until the cheese is melted.

CROUTONS.

Cut stale bread in slices one-half inch thick. Remove the crusts and cut into one-half inch cubes. Fry in hot cottolene till light brown, or put on a tin plate and bake in the oven till delicate brown.

DRESDEN PATTY CASES.

Cut stale bread in slices one and one-half inches thick. Cut rounds out by laying a tin cup over and with a sharp knife cutting around. Cut a smaller round out, leaving the sides and bottom one-third of an inch thick. Fry in hot cottolene till delicate brown. Can be filled with any soft mixture of meat or vegetables.

TOASTED BREAD CASES.

Cut the bread as for dresden patty cases and toast till delicate brown in the oven or on a toaster.

HAM TOAST.

½ c. ham.   Spk. cayenne.   1 egg.
½ tbsp. butter.   1 tsp. cream.

Mince the ham very fine. Beat the egg, add the cream, cayenne and ham. Make the toast, put the butter in a frying-pan when hot, add the ham and stir all the time till it thickens. Spread on the toast and serve.

DRIPPINGS.

Save all the scraps of fat, cut in small bits and put in a frying-pan. Pare a raw potato, cut in thin slices and add to the fat. As the fat melts pour it off through a fine sieve. Cook till the fat is light yellow. Many prefer to cover the fat with water and let the water boil away. These drippings are good to fry anything that you need a little fat for. Save some beef fat separate, and try it out alone, as directed above, and use with half lard for pastry.

BRAISED BEEF.

1 onion.   1 qt. boiling water.
2 tbsp. drippings.   1 tbsp. flour.
Boquet of mixed herbs.   1 " butter.
4 lbs. beef from the lower part of round.

Dredge the meat with salt, pepper and flour. Cut the onion into small pieces and fry it in the dripping till yellow; skim it out and put the beef into the dripping and brown it on all sides. Put the beef into a deep baking pan with the onion and the quart of boiling water. Tie the herbs in a small piece of cheese cloth and put them in the water. Cover closely and steam in a moderate oven for four hours. Baste every twenty minutes, add more water when this evaporates. When the meat is tender remove it and the bag of herbs; cook the tablespoonful of flour in the butter till brown, add the water gradually and season with salt and pepper. You may add a few mushrooms, tomato, chopped celery, or any small bit of cooked vegetables you may have to the sauce. Put the sauce over the meat and serve.

POT ROAST.

2 tomatoes, or 1 c. stewed tomatoes.
4 lbs. beef from vein, rump, or round.
1 tbsp. drippings.   1 bay leaf.
1 onion.   1 c. hot water.

Dredge the meat with salt, pepper and flour, and brown in the hot drippings. Skin the tomato, cut into quarters and put in a deep pot. Remove the meat from the drippings and lay on the tomatoes, cook the onion in the drippings, add onion, water and bay leaf to the meat and simmer, closely covered, till the meat is tender. Add a very little water as the water boils away. Season with salt and pepper. Serve hot, with the gravy thickened with a little flour, moistened in a little cold water and stirred into the tomato.

PANNED CHICKEN.

Choose young, tender chickens for this. After they are cleaned, split down the back, dredge with salt and pepper inside and out, lay them with the skin side up in a baking-pan; fold the legs over one another and skewer into shape. Dredge with flour, put small bits of butter all over the top and put in a hot oven with *no water*. After ten minutes, baste with a little hot water, in which you have dissolved a little butter. Bake until the chickens are brown all over and the joints separate easily. Baste every ten minutes. Make the gravy with a little flour, mixed smooth in a little cold water, and stirred into the liquid left in the pan. Add a little hot water if needed. Season with salt and pepper and add the giblets, which have been cooked and chopped fine.

STEWED CELERY.

1 tbsp. butter. 1 tsp. salt.
1 " flour. $\frac{1}{4}$ " white pepper.
$\frac{3}{4}$ c. milk, scalded. 1 small head of celery.

Wash and clean the celery, cut in inch lengths and cook in boiling, salted water till tender. Drain thoroughly; cook the flour and butter till smooth, add the hot milk gradually, stirring well; cook two minutes, stirring all the time; add the seasoning and celery.

RAISIN AND RICE PUDDING.

$\frac{1}{2}$ c. rice. 1 c. boiling water.
$\frac{1}{2}$ tsp. salt. 1 c. " milk.
1 c. raisins. 2 tbsp. sugar.

Wash and pick over the rice, put it with the boiling water and salt into the upper part of a double boiler; place this on the stove and boil hard ten minutes. Place over hot water, steam twenty minutes, then add the hot milk, sugar and raisins; stir well with a fork and steam thirty minutes longer. Serve hot.

LEMON SNOW.

1 qt. milk.
5 tbsp. cornstarch.
½ ssp. salt.
½ c. sugar.
Whites 4 eggs.
½ tsp. lemon.

Mix the cornstarch with a little cold milk, scald the remainder of the milk, add the cornstarch to the hot milk, stirring all the time; cook five minutes, stirring well. Add the sugar and salt; when dissolved set aside to cool. When cool add the flavoring, beat the whites stiff, and gradually pour over them the thickened milk. Put on the ice, and serve cold with cream or preserved fruit.

STRAWBERRY OR RASPBERRY SPONGE.

1 qt. berries.
½ box gelatine.
1½ c. water.
1 c. sugar.
Juice 1 lemon.
Whites 4 eggs.

Soak the gelatine in half a cup of water two hours. Mash the berries with half the sugar, and let stand half an hour. Simmer the remaining cup of water and the remaining half cup of sugar together for twenty minutes, add the gelatine; when dissolved, strain; mash the berries through a hair sieve, add them to the gelatine; add the lemon and set in a pan of ice. Stir occasionally, and when it begins to thicken, fold in lightly the well-beaten whites. Pour into a mold wet with cold water, and set on ice. Serve with cream.

SWEET OMELET.

4 eggs.
¼ ssp. salt.
1 tbsp. gran. sugar.
1 "   powd.   "

A few drops ext. of lemon.

Separate the eggs, being careful not to let any of

the yolk get into the whites. Beat the yolks with a dover beater till thick and creamy, add the gran. sugar, salt and extract. Beat the whites stiff, add the powd. sugar, beat well; pour the yolks over the whites, folding in lightly with a knife. Put a little butter on a frying-pan, when hot, see that it is melted all over the pan, put the omelet in by the teaspoonful. Cook until brown on the under side, put in the oven to set the rest for a few moments, fold over and turn out on a hot dish, and dust with powdered sugar. Score with a red-hot poker.

CUSTARD CREAM MERINGUE.

5 eggs.
3 tbsp. gran. sugar.
4 "   powd. sugar.
½ ssp. salt.
2 c. cream or milk.
¼ tsp. vanilla.

Scald the cream, beat the yolks, add the granulated sugar and the salt, pour the cream over the eggs, stirring well, return to the fire, and cook till thick, stirring all the time; add the flavoring, strain into a dish and let cool; then beat the whites stiff, add the powdered sugar gradually and pile on top of the cream, and put in a cool oven about ten minutes.

CHESTNUTS AND CREAM.

Shell the chestnuts. Pour boiling water over them and remove the inner brown skin. Boil in salted water till soft. Drain and mash through a colander, pile up in a pyramid on a glass dish; put two tablespoonfuls of sugar into one pint of cream, add a very little almond extract, only a few drops, whip the cream and pile around the chestnuts.

STUFFED APPLES.

Core and pare medium-sized tart apples, taking care to remove all the cores. Fill the cavity left by the core with the following mixture:

1½ tbsp. butter.   1 c. large white bread crumbs.
½ c. sugar.   ¼ tsp. cinnamon.
    Grated rind and juice 1 lemon.

Mix the sugar, cinnamon and rind, mix this with the crumbs; melt the butter and pour over the crumbs, tossing them with a fork. Put this mixture in the cavity, and a little on top of the apples. Squeeze a little lemon juice on top of the apples, put a teaspoonful of sugar in the spaces between the apples, and allow one teaspoonful water to two apples. Pour the water in the pan, cook in a hot oven till the apples are soft but not out of shape. Shield the crumbs at first with a piece of buttered paper or another pan, then at last brown them. Serve hot or cold, with sweetened cream or creamy sauce. They are very delicious with no sauce.

STUFFED PEARS.

Prepare the same as stuffed apples.

AMBROSIA.

6 oranges.   ½ c. grated cocoanut.
    ½ c. powdered sugar.

Peel the oranges and remove all the white skin, cut up in half-inch slices, then into small bits, removing all the hard centre. Sprinkle a little sugar over them, and set them on the ice for two hours. When ready to serve, pile on a glass dish, sift half the powdered sugar over them, cover them with the cocoanut, and sift the remainder of the sugar over the cocoanut.

SALTED ALMONDS.

Shell one-half pound of almonds. Pour boiling water over them. Let stand a few moments, put into cold water and rub off the skin. Spread on a pan; when dry, add one teaspoonful of butter, and stir on top of the stove till all are greasy, put in the oven till pale yellow, turn often. When yellow, sift with one tablespoonful of fine table salt, shake well. When cold, sift off almost all the extra salt.

SALTED PEANUTS.

May be prepared in the same way as salted almonds.

ORANGE COMPOTE.

½ c. hot water. Juice of 1 lemon.
1 pt. sugar. 9 oranges.

Boil the water and sugar, skim the syrup, add the lemon juice. Peel the oranges, removing all the white skin; cut across the middle, taking out the seeds, and drop them into the hot syrup three or four at a time. Let them scald five minutes, skim out the sections and place on a flat dish. When all are done, boil the syrup five minutes, pour over them and serve cold.

WHIPPED CREAM.

1 c. cream. ½ tsp. vanilla.
1 tbsp. sugar.

Put the cream, sugar and vanilla into a pint bowl. Set this bowl in another bowl or pan filled with ice. When very cold put the whip churn in, tilt it a little that the bottom may not rest flat on the bottom of the bowl; hold the churn firmly, with the left hand on the cover, draw the dasher up with a light, quick stroke, and push down with a hard, strong motion. Break the first bubbles that come, as they are too large; skim the froth off into a sieve stood in another bowl; use any cream that drains through from the froth to whip again.

JELLIED TRIFLE.

Whites 3 eggs. $\frac{1}{2}$ c. jelly.
3 tbsp. powd. sugar.

Beat the whites stiff. They should be fresh eggs and very cold, or they will not whip. Add the sugar gradually, then the jelly; beat well and serve in glasses.

WELSH RAREBIT.

$\frac{1}{3}$ c. cream cheese. $\frac{1}{3}$ tsp. salt.
$\frac{1}{4}$ c. cream or milk.   1 egg.
1 tsp. mustard.   A few grains cayenne.
1 " butter.   3 slices of toast.

Grate the cheese, put it with the milk on to heat; make the toast; mix the salt, pepper and mustard, add the well-beaten egg, beat well; when the cheese is melted add the egg and butter, and cook over hot water until it thickens, stirring all the time. Do not cook over 2 m., or it will curdle. Put on the toast and serve.

ODDS AND ENDS.

PICKED-UP SOUP.

1 or 2 chop bones.	½ c. pieces of meat.
1 or 2 steak "	1½ qts. water.
½ onion.	1 tsp. salt.
¼ carrot.	¼ " pepper.
¼ turnip.	¼ c. split peas.
1 stalk celery.	½ c. tomato.
1 bay leaf.	1 sprig parsley.

½ tbsp. dripping.

Put the bones, meat, salt, pepper, peas, parsley and bay leaf on to boil. Chop the vegetables fine, fry till brown in the dripping, turn into the soup. Simmer for two or three hours. Strain the tomato, strain the soup, skim off the fat, add the tomato to the soup; season with salt, pepper, and a little sugar.

WARMED-UP SALMON.

Melt a small piece of butter in a frying-pan; add one tablespoonful each of onion, carrot, turnip, and ½ tsp. salt; fry till brown, then lay in a few pieces of cooked salmon; add one-third of a cup of stock; simmer for half an hour; remove the fish, strain the gravy, season with salt, pepper, lemon juice and a little Worcester sauce. Pour over the fish and serve.

PLAIN HASH.

Equal parts of finely chopped *meat*, not fat or gristle, and cooked potatoes; cold boiled are the best, but mashed can be used. Put a little butter in a frying-pan, when hot add the hash and a very little hot water. Boil until the water is almost gone, season and serve.

VEGETABLE HASH.

Chop fine, small pieces of cabbage, beets, turnips and a little onion ; add as much potato as you have of all the others; put a little dripping in a pan, when hot add the hash, season with salt and pepper and serve.

CORNED-BEEF BALLS.

Chop the meat as fine as meal, add half the quantity of hot mashed potato ; mix thoroughly with the meat, season with a little onion juice, mustard, cayenne and salt, if needed. Shape into balls, roll in crumbs, egg and crumbs, and fry in hot cottolene.

PRESSED MEAT.

Chop any scraps of meat, which have been stewed till tender, very fine. Season highly with a little cloves, cinnamon, mace, allspice, salt, pepper and a few drops of onion juice. Add a little boiling stock, or you may boil any bones you may have a long time, and this will help it to jelly. Add the liquid to the meat, press into a square mold and set aside to cool. Cut in slices when ready to serve. You can decorate the top of the mold with rings of hard boiled egg, or a little parsley.

CORN BEEF HASH.

2 c. cooked corned beef.   1 tbsp. beef drippings.
2 c. cold boiled potatoes. Salt and pepper, if needed.

Cut the meat and potatoes into small pieces, season them, put the dripping in a frying-pan, when hot add the meat and potatoes, well mixed ; press and smooth down on the pan and cook until brown on the under side. Do not stir, but move the pan, that all may be evenly browned. Fold over carefully like an omelet and turn out on a hot platter.

CORNED BEEF HASH NO. 2.

1 c. cold corned beef. 1 tbsp. butter.
1 c. hot mashed potato. Salt and pepper, if needed.
A little bit of mustard.

Chop the corned beef as fine as meal, add the potato and melted butter and mustard and beat thoroughly. Taste and season. Make into a small, high mound, on a platter, smooth it with a knife, spread a little soft butter over it and bake in a hot oven till brown all over.

CORNED BEEF HASH NO. 3.

1 c. cooked corned beef. 1 tbsp. butter.
1 c. cold boiled potato. $\frac{1}{4}$ c. cold water.
Salt and pepper, if needed.

Chop the potato and corned beef quite fine, taste and season them; put the butter in a frying-pan; when hot add the hash and the water; boil three minutes and serve.

SCALLOPED VEAL.

Remove the bone, fat and gristle from any cold cooked veal; sprinkle a shallow dish with large, buttered bread crumbs, cover with a layer of veal, cut in thin slices, in cubes, or chopped fine, as your meat will allow; sprinkle with a little salt and pepper and pour a little veal gravy over, or a little stewed tomato, or tomato sauce. Cover with buttered crumbs and bake with the dish covered fifteen minutes, then remove the cover and brown the crumbs.

SLICED BEEF WITH TOMATO SAUCE.

1 tsp. mustard.	½ small onion.
1 tbsp. butter.	½ c. stock, or gravy.
6 tbsp. stewed tomato.	1 tbsp. Worcester sauce.
Salt and cayenne pepper.	Slices of beef or steak.

Chop the onion fine, cook it in the butter till light yellow, add the tomato gradually, then the gravy, sauce and mustard. Season with salt and cayenne and warm the slices of meat in it.

PICKED UP CHICKEN.

1 c. cold, cooked chicken.	½ tsp. lemon juice.
1 c. white sauce.	2 drops onion juice.
3 tbsp. cold, cooked cranberries.	¼ tsp. celery salt.

Make the sauce, cut the chicken into small pieces, warm it in the sauce, season with salt and pepper, if needed, add the lemon juice and celery salt, serve in toasted bread cases, or dresden patty cases, with two sprigs of parsley and one teaspoonful of cranberry on top.

COLD CHOPS WITH TOMATO SAUCE.

Prepare either tomato sauce No. 1 or 2; lay the cooked chops in a frying-pan, pour the sauce over them, let it boil gently five minutes and serve in the sauce; decorate with points of toast.

SCALLOPED HAM AND CHICKEN.

Cut equal parts of cold roast or boiled chicken and ham into cubes or small bits. Prepare some large, white, buttered bread crumbs. Make one cup of white sauce. Line a baking-dish with a thin layer of crumbs, then a layer of meat; add to the white sauce one-quarter of a teaspoonful of celery salt, or you may put a little chopped celery with the meat;

cover the meat with the sauce and cover the top with buttered crumbs. Bake, covered, for fifteen minutes, then remove the cover and brown the crumbs.

SCALLOPED TURKEY.

Cut up bits of cold, cooked turkey; if you have no gravy left, stew the bones in a very little water; strain, remove the fat and use this as gravy; put a layer of buttered crumbs in a dish, then a layer of turkey, sprinkle a little stuffing over the meat, then a little gravy; if you have very little turkey and wish to make a larger dish, you may put in a layer of oysters and sprinkle with salt, pepper, and a little lemon juice. Cover with buttered crumbs and bake, covered, for fifteen minutes, then uncover and brown the crumbs. You may use tomato sauce, or a little stewed tomato in place of gravy.

WARMED UP SWEET POTATOES.

Make one cup of white sauce; cut up into cubes or small pieces any cold, cooked sweet potatoes; add to the white sauce when hot; serve. Turnips, parsnips, carrots, cauliflower and cabbage may be done in the same way.

RICE BALLS.

Put a little cold, boiled rice into a double boiler or a steamer and warm; if very thick, you may add a teaspoonful of gravy. Add to this half the quantity of finely chopped meat. Season the whole with salt and pepper. Add to one cup of this mixture one well-beaten egg. When cold, shape into balls, the size of a large hickory nut and roll in crumbs, egg and crumbs and fry in hot cottolene.

RICE AND CHEESE.

Take a cupful of cold, boiled rice and put it in an earthen dish, with alternate layers of grated cheese. Season with a little salt and a few little bits of butter. Over one cupful of bread crumbs pour slowly one tablespoonful of melted butter, tossing the crumbs with a fork; cover the top with these crumbs. Put into one corner of the dish one cupful of milk, taking care not to wet the crumbs. Bake one-half hour. Serve hot.

RICE FRITTERS.

Add two or three tablespoonfuls of cold, boiled rice to the fritter batter and fry in hot cottolene. Sprinkle with powdered sugar.

HOMINY PUDDING.

1 c. cold cooked hominy. 3 eggs.
1 tbsp. butter. 2 c. milk.
1 " sugar. Salt to taste.

Beat the yolks, add the sugar, then the milk, pour this onto the hominy, mixing slowly with a fork, and try to free the hominy from lumps. Add the melted butter last. If the hominy has been properly salted you will need only one-half a saltspoon of salt. Bake till firm—about thirty minutes. Serve with sauce or with sugar.

OATMEAL BREAKFAST CAKES.

½ c. cooked oatmeal. 1 egg.
½ c. flour. 1 tbsp. sugar.
½ c. milk. ½ tsp. salt.
¼ tsp. Cleveland's baking-powder.

Mash the oatmeal with a fork, add the salt and sugar to it and mix thoroughly. Beat the egg, add the milk to it. Sift the flour and baking-powder into the oatmeal, add the milk, beat well, and put by the spoonful on to a well greased griddle; when one side is brown, turn over and brown the other and serve at once with syrup or sugar.

Hominy, rice, or any grain left over from the previous breakfast may be used in this way. If the grain is very soft add a little more flour. The mixture should be thick enough to drop from a spoon, not pour.

ITALIAN EGGS.

Separate the eggs very carefully, keeping each yolk in half the shell, and stand up in something to prevent it falling over. Make as many rounds of toast as you have eggs, set on a hot dish where they will keep warm. Beat the whites stiff, adding $\frac{1}{2}$ ssp. salt to every two eggs. Put a little butter in a pan; when melted all over the pan, put in the yolk of one egg very carefully, so as not to break it, and cover it at once with a heaping spoonful of the beaten whites; when cooked, lift it up carefully and lay on the round of toast. Decorate with a sprig of parsley and serve at once.

CORNSTARCH PUDDING.

1 tbsp. cornstarch. 2 eggs.
1 " powd. sugar. 1 tsp. butter.
1 c. milk. $\frac{1}{2}$ ssp. salt. 2 tbsp. gran. sugar.

Rub the cornstarch smooth in $\frac{1}{4}$ c. cold milk; add the gran. sugar and the yolks of the eggs and salt; scald the milk and pour into this; return to the fire and cook five minutes, stirring all the time. Add the butter, stir well, put in small molds, bake fifteen minutes; remove from the oven, spread with any small quantity of preserved fruit you may have; beat the whites stiff, add the powdered sugar, pile on the top and bake in a cool oven fifteen minutes.

TOMATOES AND RICE.

1 c. cold cooked rice. 1 c. stewed tomato.
1 tsp. sugar. 1 tbsp. butter.

Mix the rice, tomato and sugar, add the butter, melted, put in a baking dish, cover with large, buttered bread crumbs, and bake till the crumbs are brown.

BREAD AND CURRANT PUDDING.

1 pt. milk. 3 eggs.
3 tbsp. gran. sugar. $\frac{1}{2}$ c. currants.
2 " powd. " 1 ssp. cinnamon.
Grated rind of one lemon.
Thin slices of stale bread and butter.

Line a small, shallow baking-dish with one layer of thin slices of stale bread, buttered; mix half the gran. sugar with the cinnamon and lemon rind, and sprinkle over the bread, reserving a little for the next layer. Sprinkle half the currants over the bread. Beat the yolks of the eggs, add the half of the sugar that you did not mix with the cinnamon, add the milk to the beaten egg, and pour half of this over the bread. Add another layer of bread, sugar, cinnamon and currants, and pour on the remainder of the milk. Bake until brown—about thirty minutes; remove from the oven; beat the whites stiff, add the powd. sugar gradually, heap on the top and bake in a cool oven for fifteen minutes. Serve hot or cold.

APPLE AND RICE PUDDING.

2 apples.	1 pt. milk.
2 tbsp. rice.	2 eggs.
2 " gran. sugar.	½ tsp. lemon extract.
2 " powd. "	½ ssp. salt.

Pick over and wash the rice, and put it with the milk and salt into the double boiler, and cook thirty minutes. While this is cooking, put one pint of hot water in a granite pan on the fire, add half a cup of gran. sugar, let boil five minutes; core, pare and quarter the apples and cook in this syrup till a straw will go through them. Drain them carefully and lay in a shallow dish. Lay away the syrup in which they were cooked to stew apples or fruit in again. Beat the yolks of the eggs, add the 2 tbsp. of gran. sugar to them, stir into the rice, remove at once from the fire, add the lemon extract and pour all over the apples. Bake about thirty minutes. Beat the whites stiff, add the gran. sugar gradually, heap on the top and cook in a cool oven fifteen minutes.

APPLE BREAD AND BUTTER PUDDING.

Core, pare and halve medium-sized cooking apples. Cut slices of stale bread one-half inch thick, and out of these cut as many rounds as you have apples, and just the size of the apples. Butter the slices of bread, lay an apple on each slice and sprinkle the apple with a little sugar, in which you have mixed a little grated rind of a lemon and a little cinnamon. Put a little dab of butter on top of each apple, and bake till the apples are done; about thirty minutes. Add a little more butter when the apples are half done.

APPLES AND MERINGUE.

Put one pint of hot water and one cup of sugar on the fire, boil five minutes. Core, pare and quarter the apples, and stew in this till a straw will pierce them. Drain very dry and lay apart till cold. Pile high on a dish, beat the whites of two eggs stiff, add two tablespoons of powdered sugar gradually, a few drops of lemon extract, and pile on top of the apples.

COMPOTE OF PEARS.

Put one pint of hot water, one cup of granulated sugar, one square inch of stick cinnamon and a thin slice of lemon peel in a saucepan, and boil five minutes. Pare, core and cut the fruit into halves. Stew in the syrup till tender enough to pass a straw through them. Drain carefully, when all the fruit is cooked, boil the syrup a few minutes longer and pour it over the fruit. Serve cold.

APPLES AND CREAM.

Stew the apples as for apples for luncheon. Add 2 tbsp. of sugar to 1 c. cream, whip it thoroughly, pile the apples on a glass dish and put the cream all over.

SPONGE CAKE IN CUSTARD.

Grated rind 1 lemon.   Strawberry jam.
2 eggs.   1 tbsp. gran. sugar.
1 c. milk.   1 "   powd. "

Stale Sponge Cake.

Put a layer of stale sponge cake or lady fingers in a small, shallow dish. Spread with jam; raspberry or strawberry are the best. Scald the milk, beat the yolks of the eggs, add the gran. sugar and lemon rind, pour the milk over the eggs, pour over the cake. Bake about 20 m., till the custard is set. Remove from the oven, beat the whites stiff, add the powd. sugar, beat well; heap on the top and bake 15 m. in a cool oven.

FRIED CAKE.

Cut any stale cake into slices, beat one egg, add ½ c. milk, dip the cake into this and fry in hot cottolene. Drain on brown paper and serve hot.

CAKE FRITTERS.

Cut stale cake in slices one inch thick, and then into squares or rounds. Fry in hot cottolene until light-brown, spread with jelly or preserve, and serve hot with creamy sauce.

BANANA BLANC MANGE.

1 qt. milk. ¼ c. sugar.
4 tbsp. cornstarch. 1 tsp. vanilla.
2 or 3 bananas.

Mix the cornstarch with a little cold milk, scald the remainder, pour on to the cornstarch, stirring all the time; return to the fire and cook five minutes, stirring constantly; add the sugar. Remove from the fire, when cool add the vanilla and the bananas sliced thin, pour into cups that have been dipped into cold water. Serve very cold.

INVALID COOKING.

Only a few hints will be given here in regard to the diet for the sick, as special courses and training are given in this branch of cooking. Always consult the attending physician with regard to the food and *obey* him; relapses may occur from carelessness in this respect. Find out a number of dishes to choose from and then tax your ingenuity to the utmost to vary and tempt the appetite by a pleasing variety. Remember, it is the place of the nurse to help create an appetite by the attractiveness of the food. Serve very little at a time and in the most delicate way; choose the prettiest cup, the daintiest napkin and the smallest tray. Never take the same thing twice in succession, put it in a different dish and always serve a little less than you want the patient to take; it will generally whet the appetite to find so little. Taste every thing and see that it is palatable, before giving to the patient. Feed the patient slowly and if possible, have some little bit of pleasant news or something funny to tell them. They will relish the food more and it will do them more good. Never tell them what they are to have the next time *or they won't take it.* Surprise them with something different as often as possible. Remove every dish and particle of food from the room as soon as the patient has finished; never keep even a cracker in the room, and fruit only long enough to please the eye, then put away in a cool place. Have the food cooked by the best rules, that all the nourishment possible may be derived from it. See that the dishes to serve hot food in are warmed, and wash any delicate china yourself, that it may not be broken. Do not worry over the little nourishment taken; remember, that sometimes the system needs rest and very little food is required, but in the most digestible form; for the stomach is feeble, like the rest of the body. In building up, the system must have what has been burned up, or wasted away during sickness. Protieds from the animal kingdom, butter and cream for the fats, and starchy foods prepared so as to be easily digested, such as gruels; oxygen also must be brought as regular as the food, for if the lungs are not supplied with pure air, the food cannot give the strength to the body which it needs.

Among the best protieds are milk, beef tea, made of lean meat, juice of rare beef, squeezed out with a lemon squeezer, mutton broth, chicken broth, and a very fresh egg. Starchy foods in the form of gruels; rice will not tax the most delicate digestion, and barley is also good. Toast is considered invalid food because in the process of toasting, part of the starch is changed into dextrine, which is more easily digested; but it must be *thoroughly dried*, or it is little better than *hot bread*.

A mealy, baked potato, but no potatoes cooked in any other way.

Broiled or roasted meats, but no fried food of any kind.

The juice, but not the pulp of fruits.

HOW TO CARE FOR THE SICK.

Have every thing scrupulously neat about your-

INVALID COOKING.

self, the patient and the room. Wear some soft, washable dress, never black, as color has a great effect upon the feelings; noiseless shoes, and make yourself look as sweet and attractive as possible. It does a patient good to see any thing pretty and tidy around them.

Wipe up the dust from under the bed with a damp cloth tied over a broom. Shield the patient from all draught and the eyes from any strong light. Air all clothing thoroughly, *away from the room*, and slightly warm any change of clothing before using.

Have no flowers in the room and never use a lamp in a sick room. An open fire-place or stove is very good, giving a circulation of air. Put coal on by putting a few pieces in a paper bag and put bag and coal on together; this may be done without waking the patient.

You can wring out hot bandages by putting them in the middle of a dry towel and twisting the ends of the towel.

When you have no ice and need cool cloths, wring out of cold water and wave in some window or open door; this will prove much more grateful than when wrung out of ice water and is used in hospitals in the tropics.

OATMEAL GRUEL.

Pound a quarter of a pound of coarse oatmeal on an old bread board until it is floury. Put this into a small bowl and fill the bowl with cold water; stir thoroughly, let it settle and pour off the water, being careful not to take any of the sediment. Fill with cold water again, stir and pour off and repeat once more. Add one saltspoonful of salt and boil the water twenty minutes, stirring often. Strain, thin it with a little cream or milk and season with a little more salt, if needed; serve hot. Beef juice, beef tea, or beef extract, may be used in place of the cream.

OATMEAL GRUEL NO. 2.

2 tbsp. oatmeal.   1 ssp. salt.   1½ c. boiling water.

Put the oatmeal and salt in the boiling water and boil for forty minutes. Strain through a fine wire strainer, put on the fire again, thin it with milk or cream, bring to the boiling point and serve hot. Many people like a teaspoonful of sugar in it, but some prefer it without.

FARINA GRUEL.

1 tbsp. farina.   1 c. boiling water.
1 ssp. salt.   1 c. milk.

Mix the farina and salt, pour the boiling water on to the farina, stirring; cook ten minutes. Add the milk, boil one minute and serve hot. You may add one teaspoonful of sugar if desired.

BARLEY GRUEL.

1 tbsp. barley-flour.   1 ssp. salt.
1 c. boiling water.   1 c. milk.

Mix the barley-flour and salt with a little cold water, pour on the boiling water and boil ten minutes; add the milk, bring to the boiling point and serve. A teaspoonful of sugar may be added if desired.

ARROWROOT GRUEL.

1 tbsp. arrowroot.   1 ssp. salt.
1 c. boiling water.

Wet the arrowroot and salt with a little cold

water, pour on the boiling water, stirring; boil ten minutes, thin with a little milk if desired, and you may add a little sugar.

CRACKER GRUEL.

2 tbsp. cracker crumbs. $\frac{1}{2}$ ssp. salt.
1 c. milk.   1 c. boiling water.

Pour the water on to the crumbs slowly, stirring, add the salt, add the milk, boil 1 minute and serve.

OATMEAL MUSH.

1 c. oatmeal. $3\frac{1}{2}$ c. boiling water.
$\frac{1}{2}$ tsp. salt.

Put all in a double boiler and cook two hours. Serve with cooked apples, for invalids or children.

HOMINY MUSH.

$\frac{3}{4}$ c. hominy.   1 qt. boiling water.
1 tsp. salt.

Put in a double boiler and cook two to three hours, according to the size of the hominy.

PANADA NO. 1.

1 pt. water. $\frac{1}{2}$ c. bread crumbs.
$\frac{1}{2}$ tsp. butter.   1 level tsp. sugar.

Boil the water and crumbs for fifteen minutes, or until the mixture is perfectly smooth, stirring well; then add the butter and the sugar. You may boil half a cup of raisins in the water for half an hour, and then skim out and use it to cook with the bread, or you may use a blade of mace for the seasoning, or a little nutmeg. The butter may be omitted, if desired.

PANADA NO. 2.

Split any hard biscuits, put them in layers in a

bowl, sprinkling a little salt and sugar over each layer. Cover them with boiling water and stand the bowl in a pan of boiling water, and let stand until the crackers are clear. The crackers should be perfectly soft but unbroken, and the bowl should be tightly closed while steaming.

OATMEAL PORRIDGE.

2 tbsp. oatmeal. $\frac{1}{2}$ c. cold water.
1 pt. boiling water. $\frac{1}{4}$ tsp. salt.

Mix the oatmeal and the cold water, add the salt, pour on the boiling water and boil for forty minutes, stirring often. Serve with milk.

MILK PORRIDGE.

1 pt. milk.   1 tbsp. flour.
Salt to taste.

Rub the flour to a smooth paste, with a little cold milk. Put the remainder of the milk on the fire, and when boiling add the flour, stirring well; boil ten minutes. Season with salt, strain and serve. You may sweeten it if you prefer.

OYSTER TEA NO. 1.

Put eight freshly-opened oysters into a stew-pan, with their own liquor, and simmer for five minutes. Then strain the liquor, season with a little salt and white pepper, and serve hot, with a bit of toast.

OYSTER TEA NO. 2.

Chop eight oysters, put them on the fire, bring to a boil, simmer five minutes, strain, add a little milk; as soon as hot season with white pepper and salt, and serve. Do not boil or it will curdle.

PAN-BROILED OYSTERS.

Drain the oysters and dry thoroughly on a towel.

Have a small hot frying-pan, put a small piece of butter in; when it melts let it run all over the pan, lay in one oyster at a time, and turn immediately. Cook only three at a time, for the pan should be very hot, and the first one will be done by the time the third is put in. Serve at once on a small bit of toast.

CREAMED OYSTERS.

1 pt. oysters.
1 " cream.
Salt and pepper to taste.
1 tbsp. cornstarch.
1 blade mace.
1 tbsp. butter.

Remove all shell from the oysters by passing through the fingers. Scald the cream with the mace, cook the butter and cornstarch till smooth and frothy, add the cream slowly, stirring free from all lumps; when half the cream is used remove from the fire and give a thorough beating; add the remainder slowly, stirring well. Put the oysters in a shallow pan on the fire and cook till plump, shaking the pan so they may not burn. Drain, add to the cream, season and serve on toast or with points of toast.

ROASTED OYSTERS.

Wash the shells thoroughly. Put them in a very hot oven with the hollow side of the shell down, so as to hold the juice. When the shells open remove the upper half of the shell; season them with salt, pepper and a very little butter. Serve in their shells immediately.

CLAM BROTH.

Wash the clam shells thoroughly, put about five or six clams in a kettle, with a very little water; not over three-quarters of a cup. Boil up once, and when the shells open it is done. Do not add salt, as it is generally salt enough.

CLAM SAUCE ON TOAST.

10 clams.   ½ tbsp. butter.
½ c. liquor of clams.   ¼ tsp. lemon juice.
Salt and pepper.   ½ blade mace.

Boil the butter and the liquor, add the clams, and boil eight minutes. Add the lemon juice, season with a little salt and white pepper, and serve on toast.

BOILED RICE WITH MILK.

½ c. rice.   ⅛ tsp. salt.   2 c. milk (hot.)

Pick over and wash the rice, put it with the salt and the milk into the top of a double boiler. Steam one hour, or until each grain is soft. Serve with a little sugar.

RICE-FLOUR MILK.

¾ c. boiling milk.   1 tbsp. rice-flour.
1 tbsp. sugar.   ¼ c. cold milk.

Mix the rice-flour with the cold milk till smooth; add the sugar, pour on the boiling milk; return to the fire and cook ten minutes, stirring well. Add the flavoring and serve hot.

BISCUIT AND MILK

Split one hard water cracker in half, soak in milk for six hours, or until the biscuit is soft. Serve with a very little salt, or a little sugar.

SOFTENED BISCUITS.

Split any hard cracker in half, pour a little boiling water over it, cover, and set where it will keep warm; add a little boiling water as this is absorbed and

INVALID COOKING. 255

when the cracker is soft spread a little butter on the top and serve hot. This is very palatable.

TOAST.

Cut stale bread into slices about one-quarter of an inch thick. Put it in a toaster and put over the lids until dry, then brown over the fire. If it is not thoroughly dry it is very indigestible and butter should never be added while the toast is hot, if to serve to an invalid.

WATER TOAST.

Dip slices of dry toast into boiling salted water, allowing one-quarter of a teaspoonful of salt to one cupful of water. Spread with a little butter and serve hot.

MILK TOAST NO. 1.

Toast as directed, spread with a very little butter and pour over the slice a little hot milk in which you have put a few grains of salt. Serve very hot. The butter may be omitted if not allowed.

MILK TOAST NO. 2.

1 c. hot milk. $\frac{1}{2}$ ssp. salt.
1 tsp. cornstarch. $\frac{1}{2}$ tbsp. butter.

Melt the butter in a small pan, add the dry cornstarch and salt, cook till smooth and frothy; add the hot milk slowly, stirring well; when one third of the milk is used give a thorough beating, add the remainder of the milk; pour between each slice of toast and over the top.

CUSTARD TOAST.

$1\frac{1}{2}$ c. hot milk. Yolks of 2 eggs.
$\frac{1}{2}$ ssp. salt. 1 tsp. sugar.
Slices of toast.

Make the toast, beat the eggs, add the sugar and the salt; pour the hot milk on to the eggs, stirring well; return to the fire and cook till thick as cream, stirring all the time. Strain, add a little flavoring and pour over the toast. This may be served cold, if desired. You may also leave out the sugar if you prefer.

RAW BEEF SANDWICHES.

Cut stale bread into slices one-quarter of an inch thick. Remove all crust; cut into two inch squares. Toast till dry and delicate brown; spread with thin layer of the scrapings from a small piece of rare, juicy, tender beef. Season with a little salt, white pepper; cover with another piece of toast and serve while the toast is hot. These are very delicious and can be given to children when they refuse meat.

TOASTED CRACKERS.

Lay thin crackers on a toaster, or on a tin pan in the oven and toast until crisp. If butter is allowed you may spread a very little over them before toasting and toast till the crackers are perfectly dry. If the butter is merely melted on the top of the crackers it is very indigestible; but if you keep them in the oven long enough they will be perfectly dry and crisp and *very delicious*.

CRACKERS AND MARMALADE.

Put the crackers on a tin plate in the oven for a few minutes. Spread with a little butter and then a thin layer of orange marmalade between; set in the oven for a few moments.

INVALID COOKING.

BEEF TEA.

1 pt. cold water. $\frac{1}{2}$ tsp. salt.
1 lb. beef off the top of the round.

Put the water and salt into the top of a double boiler, scrape the meat off until you have nothing left but the tough membrane. Put the meat as you scrape it into the water. Let it soak for two hours, then put over hot water and cook thirty minutes. Press through a strainer. Remove the fat, by laying unglazed, coarse brown paper on top to absorb it.

BEEF TEA (bottled).

$\frac{1}{2}$ lb. beef off the top of the round.
1 c. cold water. $\frac{1}{8}$ tsp. salt.

Cut off everything but the lean fibre, cut into very small pieces, put in a glass jar, and cover with the water; add the salt, cover the bottle, and set in a pan of cold water; heat the water gradually, but do not boil it; let it remain in hot water for one and one-half hours, strain out the juice by pressing the meat.

BEEF JUICE.

1 lb. beef off the top of the round.
$\frac{1}{8}$ tsp. salt.

Cut off all fat, cut the meat in very small pieces, put in a bottle, cover and stand in a pan of cold water; heat gradually, but do not boil. Let it stand in hot water for one hour, strain out the juice by pressing the meat. This will make about three tablespoonfuls of juice.

BEEF BROTH.

1 lb. beef off the top of the round.
1 pt. cold water. $\frac{1}{4}$ tsp. salt.

Chop the meat very fine, put it with the salt into the cold water, let stand a half hour, put on the stove, heat gradually and simmer closely covered for two hours. Strain through a very coarse strainer, remove the fat, season, and serve hot.

MUTTON BROTH.

1 qt. cold water. $\frac{1}{4}$ tsp. salt.
1 lb. mutton, from the neck.

Remove the skin and fat and cut the meat into small pieces, and break the bones; put the meat, bones and salt into water, heat slowly, simmer for three hours. Remove the fat and the bones, season, and serve hot. If you have time, allow it to get cold, then you can remove all the fat. A little barley or rice may be cooked in the broth.

CHICKEN BROTH.

Select a fowl, not a young chicken. Prepare the chicken for cooking, cut into small pieces, put in a saucepan and cover with cold water; add one-half teaspoonful of salt. Heat gradually and simmer for three hours, keeping it closely covered. You may add a little barley or rice when you put it on, and serve a little of it and a few bits of chicken with the broth.

FARINA CUSTARD.

2 c. milk. $\frac{1}{4}$ c. sugar.
3 tbsp. farina. 2 eggs.
$\frac{1}{2}$ tsp. vanilla. $\frac{1}{2}$ ssp. salt.

Scald the milk, beat the eggs, add the sugar and salt; mix the farina with a quarter of a cup of cold milk, add to the eggs, pour on the milk, stirring well. Return to the fire and cook eight minutes, stirring all the time. Add the vanilla, turn into little molds, which have been dipped in cold water and set aside to harden. Serve very cold, with strawberry or raspberry preserve, or custard sauce.

CHICKEN CUSTARD.

1 c. chicken broth.   Yolks 3 eggs.

Scald the broth, beat the yolks, pour the broth on to them, stirring well; return to the fire and cook till slightly thickened, stirring all the time. Salt to taste, strain, and serve cold.

BEEF TEA CUSTARD.

2 eggs.   1 c. cold beef tea.
Salt and pepper.

Scald the beef tea, beat the eggs, pour the beef tea on to the eggs, taste it and season, put into buttered cup and bake in a pan of hot water about thirty minutes.

TAPIOCA CREAM.

2 c. milk.   2 tbsp. gran. sugar.
¼ c. tapioca.   2 eggs.
½ ssp. salt.   ½ tsp. vanilla.

Soak the tapioca for four or five hours in cold water, enough to cover. Drain off all the water if there is any left, and put into a double boiler with the milk, and cook, stirring all the time till clear. Beat the yolks and the sugar, add the salt; add this to the tapioca, and boil one minute, stirring all the time. Remove from the fire, beat the whites stiff, fold in lightly, add the flavoring, and put in small glasses to cool.

ORANGE CREAM.

½ box gelatine.
1 c. sugar.
¾ c. orange juice.
2 c. cream.
2½ c. milk.
Yolks of 5 eggs.

Soak the gelatine in half a cup of milk one hour. Scald the remainder of the milk; beat the eggs, add the sugar, pour the milk on to them, stirring well; return to the fire and cook till a little thicker than cream, stirring all the while. Remove from the fire, add the gelatine; when dissolved strain, and when cold, add the orange juice, strained through a sieve. Set in a pan of ice, stir occasionally; whip the cream and when the jelly begins to thicken fold the cream in lightly; turn into molds dipped in cold water. Serve plain, or with whipped cream.

CREAM CORNSTARCH PUDDING.

1 c. milk.
¼ c. sugar.
½ tsp. lemon extract.
1 egg.
2 level tbsp. cornstarch.

Mix the cornstarch with a little cold milk, scald the remainder of the milk; beat the egg, add the sugar to it, add this to the cornstarch; pour the boiling milk on to the cornstarch, return to the fire and cook five minutes, stirring all the time. Add the flavoring, turn into small molds, wet in cold water. Set on the ice to harden; serve with custard sauce, flavored with lemon, or it is very nice plain.

ARROWROOT BLANC MANGE.

1 c. boiling milk.
2 tsp. sugar.
1½ tbsp. arrowroot.
Flavoring.
¼ c. cold milk.

Rub the arrowroot smooth in the cold milk, add

the sugar, pour the boiling milk over it, return to the fire and cook five minutes stirring all the time; add the flavoring. Set in small cups which have been dipped in cold water; serve cold, with cream.

TAPIOCA BLANC MANGE.

½ c. tapioca.   1½ tbsp. sugar.
1½ c. boiling milk.   Flavoring.

Soak the tapioca in cold water (enough to cover) for four hours, or over night is better. Then stir in the boiling milk, the tapioca and the water in which it was soaked. Add the sugar and boil very slowly till the tapioca is perfectly clear. This will depend on how long you have soaked it. Take off and flavor and set aside to cool. If the invalid can have it, strawberry preserves with this is delicious.

RICE CUSTARD.

¼ c. sugar.   ½ ssp. salt.
1 pt. hot milk.   2 eggs.
½ c. cold cooked rice.

Put the rice and salt into the milk and soak until every grain is distinct. Separate the eggs, beat the yolks with the sugar, add the rice and milk to them, return to the pan and cook till the eggs are thickened like custard. While still hot, beat the whites, fold them in lightly and set away to cool. Or you may leave the whites until the custard is cold, then beat them up stiff, add one and one-half tablespoonfuls of powdered sugar to them, heap on the top of the pudding and brown in the oven. Serve cold, either way.

JELLIED RICE.

2½ c. milk.   1 tbsp. gelatine.
3 eggs (yolks.)   ½ c. cream.
3 tbsp. rice.   3 tbsp. sugar.
A few drops of vanilla extract.

Soak the gelatine in ¼ c. milk 1 h. Wash the rice and steam in 1 c. milk 30 m. Put the remaining 1¼ c. milk in a double boiler; when scalded, beat the yolks, add 2 tbsp. sugar and pour the hot milk over them; return to the boiler and cook till thick as cream, stirring all the time; remove at once from the fire, add the gelatine and remainder of the sugar. When dissolved, strain and set away to cool. When cold, add the vanilla and rice, whip the cream and stir in lightly and set in a mold to harden. Serve with or without preserved fruit.

FARINA BLANC MANGE.

2 c. milk.   2 tbsp. farina.
2 eggs.   ½ c. sugar.
¼ tsp. lemon.   ½ ssp. salt.

Wet the farina with a little cold milk, add the salt; scald the remainder of the milk, beat the yolks, add the sugar to them. Stir the farina into the milk, cook fifteen minutes, stirring often; add the yolks and boil two minutes longer. Remove from the fire, add the flavoring and, lastly, the well beaten whites, folded in lightly. Pour into molds which have been wet in cold water; and set aside to cool. Serve with sugar and cream.

CURRANT ICE.

1 c. red currant juice.   1 c. sugar.   1 c. water.

Mix; when the sugar is dissolved, freeze.

FROZEN BEEF TEA.

Take one pint of any kind of good beef tea, season to taste, and freeze.

JELLY AND ICE.

Fill a glass half full of finely chipped ice, add the same quantity of an acid jelly, such as currant or grape, broken into small bits, stir thoroughly and serve at once. This is very refreshing for fever, and quite harmless.

TO PREPARE AN ORANGE.

Remove all the yellow skin and as much as possible of the white skin. With a very sharp knife cut from the outside through a section to the middle of the orange; turn the soft inside part of the section out, taking care not to cut the dividing membrane. Take the next section, and follow right round the orange; sprinkle with sugar and mix a little chipped ice with it. Serve at once.

COMPANY.

When at last the deed is done and the day is set, begin to plan and lay out your work. As you think of little things to be done, make a note of them. An excellent way is to jot under headings of different days the work to be done on them. Look over your table linen and have it laundered the week before, not only to lighten the wash, but because it is sure to rain, and the table-cloth be badly done! Have any little draperies, covers or towels that you need, clean, laid in a *convenient place*, but *not* where you will forget where they are! The *week before* see that the dress you wish to wear is in *perfect order*, with the laces or fixings *tacked in* and choose a dress that you can get into *quickly*. See that there are plenty of pins and hair pins in the cushions. Look over and have the silver cleaned, and the china washed a day or so before. Have all sweeping done the day before, and everything thoroughly dusted, that it may need but little time to go over it on that day.

In preparing the menu, select dishes which under the most unfavorable circumstances you are *sure* can be turned out satisfactory; for as Dr. Talmage says: "Stoves belong to a fallen race, and the best of them sometimes proves tricky. Sometimes they fly into a hot temper and burn things up, and sometimes they will pout for half an hour, because a green chip or unseasoned stick of wood is thrown at them.

The best dispositioned stove will sometimes refuse to broil or stew, or bake, or frizzle! You coax it in every possible way. You reason with it and tell it how important it is that it does its duty, for company has come or a departing guest must meet the train, and you are too tired to bother any longer, and all it does is to sputter!"

Never attempt anything *new*. Try it two or three times before. If there is anything particularly nice that you know how to make, choose *that* as one of the dishes, unless it requires too much time at the last.

Read over carefully each recipe and make a note of each item on your marketing list, even to a sprig of parsley; and do not cross them out until *you see them in the house*. Send all the groceries you can, home the day before and ask if the other articles on your list will be in market on that day. Allow a little extra time for some one to go for things which have been ordered but "have'nt come."

Make a point to see that the children have three wholesome meals at their regular time; thin crackers put in the oven till crisp, with a glass of milk and a cookey, are an easy supper. Keep all sweetmeats and dainties, as much as possible, out of sight; do not bribe them with "bits" and "a taste" all day long, or they will be fretful and sick by night. If they should seem to be ailing, as they often do on that day, *don't worry;* give them the best thing you know for them and try to get some good samaritan to come in and stay with them until you are relieved. Probably they'll be all right by the following day. As early as possible lay out all the dishes on a table near at hand and have them labeled for the different courses and go over them slowly with the servant who is to have charge of them. Have a list of the dishes to be served *written plainly* and tack it up *yourself* in the most convenient place; one list in the kitchen and one in the serving pantry.

Try and eat your meals, or at least drink a cup of tea or coffee. A glass of milk or a cup of tea taken just before they arrive will often relieve nervousness. When it is all over remember only the pleasant part and forget the mistakes that seemed so large to you and perhaps were not seen at all by others.

TO PREPARE CANNED VEGETABLES.

Open the can, drain off all the liquid, turn the vegetable into a colander and rinse thoroughly in cold water. Put in a saucepan, cover with cold water and bring to the boiling point. Throw this water off immediately and season the vegetable with butter, salt and pepper. The two cold waters help to remove the taste of the tin.

TO CLEAN CURRANTS.

Rub with flour, put in a colander and shake the stems off; rinse three times in cold water. Dry in a towel.

TO STONE RAISINS.

Pour boiling water over them, rub between the fingers until the seeds push out.

TO PREPARE LETTUCE.

Break off all the defective leaves and use these for the inside of the salad, reserving the whole leaves for decorating and serving the salad on. Break off each leaf with the hands, wash carefully and lay in very cold water till needed. When ready to use take each leaf up separately, shake gently, dry between two towels and serve in a bowl. Never cut it apart with a knife.

TO PREPARE CUCUMBERS.

Choose the small, green and white ones, with no yellow, and have them firm to the touch. Take off a thick paring, slice thin and lay in cold water for an hour. Just before serving, drain and serve on ice.

TO PREPARE CELERY.

Select the tender, white stalks, remove the green part and lay aside for stews or soup. Wash thoroughly and lay in cold water for several hours before using. Do not clean it until it is crisp. You may serve each stalk separate, or a few stalks on one root.

QUESTIONS ON COURSE A.

LESSON I.

1. What is air composed of?
2. What is fuel composed of?
3. When oxygen combines with fuel what is the result?
4. Why must we have the draughts open when starting a fire?
5. When can we close them?
6. What does the blue flame show?
7. How do you fix a fire to leave for several hours?
8. When do you blacken the stove?
9. When do you polish the stove?

LESSON II.

1. Why do we need food?
2. How may food be classified?
3. What do nitrogeneous foods supply?
4. What do carbonaceous foods supply?
5. Of what use is water as food?
6. What minerals are found in the body?
7. What is albumen, and where found in egg, meat, flour, milk, peas and beans?
8. What is water composed of?
9. What is boiling?
10. What effect does boiling have upon water?
11. What effect has cold water on starch?
12. What effect has hot water on starch?
13. What effect has cold water on albumen?
14. What effect has hot water on albumen?

LESSON III.

1. What is the difference between boiling and simmering?
2. What effect has long continued slow cooking on the fibres of meat?
3. Where ought the nutriment to be in soup?
4. What effect has cold water on meat?
5. What effect has hot water on meat?
6. What kind of food is best simmered?
7. What cuts are best for soup?

LESSON IV.

1. How many ways are there of steaming?
2. What is a double boiler?
3. How can you make one?
4. At what temperature must the water be kept in the under pan?
5. In steaming, why must you keep the cover on tight?
6. What effect will cold air have on a steamed pudding or bread?
7. How do you steam grains?
8. What is the third way of cooking meat in water?
9. Why do you fry the meats for stews?
10. What cuts are best for stews?
11. What is baking-powder made of?
12. What chemical change takes place when baking-powder is used?
13. What does carbonic acid gas do to food?

LESSON V.

1. What kind of fire do you need for roasting?
2. Why do you not put water in the pan for roasting?
3. What does salt do to the juices of meat?
4. What does the intense heat do to the meat?
5. Where do you want the juices of the meat in roasts?

6. What cuts are best for roasts?
7. What are the principal causes of decomposition of food?
8. What ought you to do with meat or fish as soon as they come from the market?
9. Why do you not salt meat or fish until just before using?
10. How often ought you to look over the perishable food?
11. What can you do with spotted fruit?

LESSON VI.

1. What is broiling?
2. Do you need tough or tender meat to broil?
3. How often do you turn it while broiling?
4. What is pan broiling?
5. What is digestion?
6. Where does the system draw from for all its needs?
7. Where does the first part of digestion take place?
8. Where does the second part of digestion take place?
9. Where does the third part of digestion take place?
10. How many digestive juices are there?
11. Where is saliva found?
12. On what food does it act?
13. Where is gastric juice found?
14. On what does it act?
15. Where are the bile and pancreatic juices found?
16. On what do they act?
17. Where is the intestinal juice found?
18. On what does it act?

LESSON VII.

1. What is frying?
2. How do you use cottolene?
3. How do you prepare lard?
4. How do you prepare beef dripping?
5. What is the test of fat for frying?

6. What do you drain all fried food on?
7. When the blood enters the lungs what does it meet there that burns up the impurities?
8. How is the waste of the system thrown off?
9. What do we throw off at every breath?
10. Is carbonic acid gas poisonous?

LESSON VIII.

1. What grain makes the most perfect bread?
2. What is yeast?
3. What does it need in order to grow?
4. What is the effect of hot liquid added to yeast?
5. What is the first change in the flour after the yeast begins to grow?
6. What is the sugar changed into?
7. If the alcoholic fermentation is not checked what acid will be formed?
8. What gas do we obtain by using yeast?
9. As the bread is baked what takes place in the yeast? the starch? the alcohol?
10. Why do we knead the bread after rising?
11. What temperature should the bread be kept in during the first rising? During the second rising?
12. How can you make the crust crisp or soft?

LESSON IX.

1. How are starchy foods best prepared for an invalid?
2. In what form is it best to give fat?
3. What is needed for the lungs?
4. What does the oxygen do to the impurities in the blood?
5. What are the best protieds for the sick?

6. When is toast digestible?
7. What are nutritious foods?
8. Why should food be cooked by the best rules?
9. How should food be served?
10. When does digestion begin?
11. How should the sick room, the nurse and the patient be kept?
12. What foods should be avoided?
13. Why do you not *boil* tea?

LESSON X.

1. How many motions are there used to mix food?
2. When do you "stir" food?
3. When do you "beat" food?
4. When do you "fold" food?
5. What raises an omelet?
6. What raises a cake?

7. How often should the refrigerator be washed out?
8. In what part of the refrigerator should milk and butter be kept in? Meat? Fish?
9. How can you keep lemons and cranberries?
10. How do you prepare drippings?
11. How do you scrape dishes?
12. What kind of water do you use to wash them?
13. When do you dry them?
14. What do you do with greasy pans?
15. How do you wash dover egg beaters?
16. How do you wash a tea pot?
17. How do you wash the sink?

QUESTIONS ON COURSE B.

LESSON I.

1. How can you tell that fish is fresh?
2. What ought to be done to meat or fish as soon as they come from the market?
3. Which is the richer fish, bluefish or cod? And why?
4. What kind of an oven do we need for baking?
5. Should meat and fish be placed in a very hot oven?
6. Why should no water be put in the pan at first?
7. What is basting?
8. Why do we use lemon or sauces with fish?

LESSON II.

1. How can you tell good poultry?
2. Why do we put meat for boiling into hot water?
3. What effect has rapid boiling on the fibres of meat?
4. What effect has simmering on the fibres of meat?
5. Why do we use soda with molasses?

6. Why should we not move a cake while it is rising?
7. What will cause a cake to fall while baking?
8. Should a cake be left in the pan after baking? And why not?
9. What is the best thing to do with a loaf cake just baked?

LESSON III.

1. What effect has hot water on yeast, and why?
2. What is the cause of bread or rolls turning sour?
3. What is best to cover them with while rising?
4. How hot should the oven be for rolls?
5. Give the order in which you make white sauce?
6. Why is it best not to pare apples till ready to use them?

LESSON IV.

1. What are oysters composed of?
2. Are they economical or expensive food?
3. How should they be cooked to be digested?

QUESTIONS ON LESSONS. 271

4. Why is it best to heat milk in a double boiler?
5. At what temperature does albumen coagulate?
6. Why do you not pour eggs into hot milk for custard?
7. How can you bring a custard back that has curdled?

LESSON V.

1. Why do we beat air into an omelet?
2. Is albumen digestible when overdone?
3. How are doughs raised?
4. Why should they be cooked as soon as wet?
5. Why must you never take the cover off while steaming a pudding or bread?
6. What kind of water do you add as it boils away?
7. How do you clean currants?
8. "   "   " stone raisins?
9. What kind of suet do you need for suet pudding?

LESSON VI.

1. How do you clean a chicken?
2. What must you be careful not to break?
3. How do you skewer a chicken for roasting?
4. What do you put on it before putting in the oven?
5. What can you use if you have no chicken fat?
6. What is requisite for a good salad?
7. In what order do you mix a cake containing butter?
8. What is beating?
9. "   " stirring?
10. "   " folding?
11. Why do you beat a cake?

LESSON VII.

1. What are the proportions of ice and salt used for freezing?
2. Should the crank be turned fast or slow to produce a smooth, fine cream?
3. Should all the ice water be kept drained off all the time?
4. Is it best to beat sponge cake much or little, and why?
5. What effect has heat upon air?
6. What effect would stirring have after beating?

LESSON VIII.

1. Give the courses in their order for a luncheon.
2. Where do you put the flowers?
3. How do you lay the knives, forks and spoons?
4. Where do you place the tumblers, butter plates, salt and pepper?
5. Where do you put the napkins?
6. How do you place the chairs?
7. On which side of the person serving should the waitress stand?
8. On which side do you pass the dishes to each person?
9. How do you remove a plate with a knife and fork on it?
10. What do you remove before brushing off the crumbs?

LESSON IX.

1. What do you need to make good pastry?
2. What kind of an oven to bake it?
3. Should the pastry be very cold when placed in the oven?
4. Where should the heat be the greater, under or on top of the pie?
5. What is best to mix it with?
6. How do you roll it out and why?
7. Do you grease the pan or not?
8. What is the test of fat for frying oysters?

LESSON X.

1. What is the process of making mayonnaise?

2. Why does it ever curdle?
3. What is a sure way to bring it back?
4. When should you mix mayonnaise with the salad, and why?
5. How do you make sandwiches?
6. Do you ever boil gelatine, and why not?
7. How do you make soft custard?

QUESTIONS ON COURSE C.

LESSON I.

1. How do you boil a lobster?
2. How long after boiling must a lobster be used?
3. What is the reason that croquettes break?
4. How should food to be fried be prepared?
5. Why should the egg entirely coat the fried food?
6. What is the test of fat for croquettes?
7. How do you add whipped cream to melted gelatine?
8. Why do you cook the flour and the butter in thick soups?

LESSON II.

1. Why do you not boil milk after adding salmon, lobster, asparagus?
2. What is meant by flaking fish?
3. How do you make delicious, light, mashed potatoes?
4. What is a purée?

LESSON III.

1. How do you prepare fillets of fish?
2. How do you boil spinach and why?
3. How do you add oil to sauces?
4. How much water do you add to one egg for breading and why?
5. Do you beat or stir waffles just before cooking and why?
6. What do you grease a waffle iron with?

LESSON IV.

1. How can you use stale bread?
2. What are the tests of fat to fry bread cases? Apple fritters?
3. What do you add to fritter batter for fruit? For fish?
4. What do you drain all fried food on and why?
5. How can you warm up bits of cold ham, veal, chicken, fish?

LESSON V.

1. Should veal be well cooked or rare?
2. What meats are best served rare?
3. How do you cook spaghetti?
4. How do you cook flour and butter and why?
5. In adding hot liquid to sauces should you stir or not and why?
6. How can you decorate with icing or meringue?

LESSON VI.

1. Do omelets require an intense heat or not?
2. How should they be put together?
3. How should they be put in the pan?
4. How soon cooked after beating?
5. What kind of a fire for baking a loaf cake?
6. What part of the oven do you put it in at first?
7. When is it likely to fall?
8. When is it safe to move it?
9. When can you tell that it is done?

LESSON VII.

1. What kind of crumbs are best for croquettes?

2. What kind for covering made up dishes?
3. What proportion of butter to 1 c. crumbs.
4. How do you put it on them?
5. Should crumbs be seasoned and what with?
6. How do you make café parfait?
7. Should maccaroons be stale or fresh for baskets?

LESSON VIII.

1. How do you clarify soup?
2. Why does the albumen clear it?
3. How do you use a cutlet mold?
4. What are scalloped dishes and what can they be made of?
5. Give the order of courses for a dinner?
6. What is an entree?
7. What are the proportions for cafe noir?
8. When should salad be mixed?

LESSON IX.

1. How can you serve fruit?
2. Out of what can you make baskets?
3. What are the principal points to be observed in making good pastry?
4. How many layers on the edge of tarts?
5. How long do you bake a meringue and in what kind of an oven?

LESSON X.

1. What are sweetbreads?
2. Where found?
3. How do you prepare them before using?
4. How long may they be kept?
5. What do you cut them with?
6. What is larding?
7. What kind of meats do we lard?
8. What kind of pork used?
9. What does soufflé mean?
10. How should a soufflé be put into the dish?
11. In what kind of an oven?
12. When can you tell that it is done?

INDEX.

	PAGE		PAGE
Introduction.		Sautéing	50
Courses		Larding	51
" A	13	Stirring, beating, folding	51
" B	15	Bread crumbing	52
" C	17	Boning	53
Mottoes	19	Care of food	56
" course A	19		
" " B	21		
" " C	23	**SOUPS.**	
How to use this book	25	Soup	64
Abbreviations	26	" clam	73
Table of measures and weights	26	" cream of asparagus	71
Time-table for cooking	27	" left over	68
Fire	29	" macaroni	68
" making and care of	30	" mock bisque	70
Food	32	" oyster	72
" nitrogenous	33	" picked up	236
" carbonaceous	33	" potato	69
Fats and oils	35	" stock	64
DIGESTION.		" white stock	65
Digestion	36	" split pea	69
Saliva	36	" tomato	69
Gastric juice	37	" to clarify	66
Bile	37	" velvet	72
Pancreatic	37	" vegetable	68
Intestinal	38	Puree of salmon	74
Nutritious foods	39	Bisque of lobster	74
Innutritious	39	Consomme	70
Daily requirement of food	40	Bouillon	71
		Julienne	71
COOKING.		**FISH.**	
Cooking	42		
Boiling	42	Fish	76
" water	42	" baked	77
" meats	43	" " stuffing for	78
" vegetables	44	" boiled	78
" grains	44	" balls	79
Simmering	44	" creamed salt	80
Steaming	44	" fried	78
Roasting	45	" " cod	79
Broiling	46	" au gratin	80
" pan	47	" " " No. 2	81
Braising	48	" picked up salt cod	80
Frying	48	" scalloped	80
" to prepare fat for	49	" turbans of	81
" test of fat for	50	" " with oysters	82

	PAGE		PAGE
Fish, to clean a	77	Beef, braised	228
Blanquette of salmon	81	" stew with dumplings	92
Warmed up "	236	" roast	91
SHELL FISH.		" " gravy for	91
		" " pot	229
Salmon timbales	83	" raw, sandwiches	256
Oysters	84	" sliced, with tomato sauce	239
" balls	82	" steak	92
" broiled	85	" " Hamburgh	92
" creamed	85	" to choose	90
" fricasseed	85	" hash	236
" Huître a la Dauphine	86	Yorkshire pudding	91
" little pigs in blankets	86	Drippings	228
" scalloped	85		
" to prepare	84	MUTTON AND LAMB.	
" raw	84	Mutton and lamb	96
LOBSTER.		" boiled	96
		" " gravy	97
Lobster	86	" chops	97
" to boil	86	" " pan broiled	97
" creamed	87	" " en papilote	98
" cutlets	88	" " with tomato	
" croquettes	88	sauce	239
" deviled	87	Mutton scalloped	99
" to open	87	" rechauffé	100
" to select	86	" roast	96
" sauce	115	" to choose	96
" salad	163	Lamb chops	97
CRABS AND SCALLOPS.		" " breaded with stuffed tomatoes	97
Crabs	88		
" to boil	89	" boned leg	99
" soft shell	89	" crown of	98
" deviled	89	Minced meat on toast	99
" broiled	89	Scotch broth	100
Scallops	88	Cottage pie	99
MEAT.		VEAL AND PORK.	
Meat	90	Veal	101
" pressed	237	" roast	101
Beef	90	" cutlets	101
" a la mode	94	" scalloped	238
" corned	93	" scalloped, a la provencale	101
" " hash	237	Casserole of mock sweetbreads	102
" " " No. 2	238	Roast pig	102
" " " No. 3	238	" " stuffing for	103
" " balls	237	Pork	102
" " croquettes	237	" roast	103
" fillet of, larded	93	" and beans	103
" frizzled	94	" tenderloin	103
" dumplings	93	" chops	103

	PAGE		PAGE
Ham, boiled	104	Sauce, parsley	114
" and eggs	104	" shrimp	114
" toast	228	" tomato No. 1	115
" creamed	104	" " " 2	115
Liver and bacon	105	" tartar	116
To try out lard	105	" " mayonnaise	117
		" romoulade	117
POULTRY AND GAME.		" white	113
Poultry	106	SWEETBREADS.	
" to truss and dress	106	Sweetbreads	118
" to choose	106	" broiled	119
Chicken roast	107	" and bacon	119
" " stuffing for	108	" creamed	118
" giblet gravy	108	" in cases	118
" boiled	108	" casserole of mock	102
" broiled	108	" larded	119
" fricassee	109	" to prepare	118
" " gravy for	109	VEGETABLES.	
" casserole of rice and	109		
" creamed	110	Vegetables	120
" Hollandaise	110	" a la jardiniere	130
" with mushrooms	110	" boiled	44
" picked up	239	" green	125
" sauté	110	" hash	237
" scalloped, ham and	239	" to prepare canned	268
To clean giblets	107	Asparagus	126
Panned chicken	229	Beans, string	125
Roast turkey	108	" lima	128
Scalloped turkey	240	Beets	126
Roast duck	111	Brussels sprouts in cream	129
" goose	111	Cabbage	126
Larded grouse	111	" a la creme	127
Bread sauce for larded grouse	112	Cauliflower, boiled	127
Quail	112	" au gratin	127
		" border of	127
MEAT AND FISH SAUCES.		Corn on the cob	128
Sauces	113	Egg plant, fried	139
" brown	113	Peas	125
" " mushroom	114	Spinach	125
" " piquante	114	" a la creme	125
" bechamel	116	Turnips	123
" cream	113	" scalloped	124
" " for croquettes	169	Tomatoes, raw	128
" caper	114	" stewed	129
" currant jelly, for mutton	114	" scalloped	129
" drawn butter	114	" stuffed	129
" egg	114	Onions, boiled	128
" Hollandaise	116	Succotash	128
" lobster	115	Macaroni	131
" Maître d'Hotel	117	" and cheese	131
" oyster	114	Spaghetti	132

13

THE YOUNG COOK'S GUIDE.

	PAGE
Celery, stewed	230
Mushrooms	130
" stewed	131
" baked	130

POTATOES.

Potatoes	120
" boiled	120
" " sweet	123
" a la Maître d'Hotel	123
" balls	121
" " in cream	122
" baked	120
" cakes	121
" creamed	121
" escaloped sweet	121
" Franconia	122
" fried	122
" " No. 2	122
" Lyonnaise	122
" mashed	120
" rice	121
" sauted	122
" sweet, fried	123
" " warmed up	240

GRAINS.

Grains	133
Oatmeal	133
" breakfast cakes	241
" gruel	249
" " No. 2	250
" mush	251
" porridge	252
Hominy	133
" breakfast cakes	241
" griddle "	136
" fried	134
" pudding	241
Cracked wheat	134
Buckwheat cakes	136
Rice	134
" apples and	244
" boiled	134
" " with milk	254
" balls	240
" breakfast cakes	241
" custard	263
" "	179
" croquettes	171

	PAGE
Rice and cheese	241
" fritters	241
" flour-milk	254
" griddle cakes	136
" jellied	264
" pudding, creamed	179
" steamed	134

GRIDDLE CAKES AND WAFFLES.

Batters	135
Griddle cakes	136
" " rice	136
" " hominy	136
" " buckwheat	136
Pancakes	136
Hominy breakfast cakes	241
Oatmeal " "	241
Waffles	137
" syrup for	193
" yeast	137

BREAD.

Bread	138
" baking	140
" made with water	141
" " " milk	142
" " " potatoes	142
" graham	142
" corn	149

ROLLS, MUFFINS, GEMS.

Rolls	143
" crescent	143
" Parker House	144
" Swedish	144
" twin	143
" White Mountain	144
" twists	145
Gems	148
" egg	149
" graham	150
Biscuits	147
" baking-powder	147
" drop	148
Muffins	151
" breakfast	150
" quick	150
" yeast	151
" corn meal	149

INDEX.

	PAGE
Sally lunn	151
" " yeast	152
Bunns	145
" currant	145
" raisin	146

EGGS.

	PAGE
Eggs	153
" baked	154
" soft boiled	153
" hard	153
" creamed	157
" dropped	153
" for breakfast	159
" poached	158
" Italian	242
" scrambled	154
" stuffed	156
" Spanish	157
" in tomato	158
" " dressed patty cases	158
" salad	164
" with cheese	158
Omelet, plain	154
" No. 2	155
" No. 3	155
" creamy	155
" orange	156
" ham	155
" soufflé	156
" sweet	231
Birds' nest	157
Welsh Rarebit	

SALADS AND SANDWICHES.

	PAGE
Salads	160
" chicken	162
" egg	164
" lettuce	162
" lobster	163
" Marguerite	164
" tomato	164
" " baskets	164
" sweetbread	164
" vegetable	163
" potato	162
Dressing, French	161
" boiled	161
" Mayonnaise	160
" " tartar	162

	PAGE
Sandwiches	166
" celery	166
" cheese	167
" French	167
" salad	166
" ham and chicken	167
" ginger	167

CROQUETTES.

Croquettes	168
" thick cream sauce for	169
" chicken	169
" codfish	170
" lobster	170
" " cutlets	170
" potato	171
" rice	171
" corned beef	171
" salmon	170
" sweetbread	171

FRITTERS.

Fritters	173
" batter	173
" apple	174
" clam	173
" corn	173
" game	173
" oyster	173
" orange	174

PUDDINGS AND DESSERTS.

Puddings	175
" apple and rice	244
" " bread and butter	244
" baked huckleberry	182
" boiled "	182
" bread, French	179
" " lemon	177
" " and currant	243
" cabinet	184
" chocolate	181
" cottage	181
" cream cornstarch	262
" " rice	179
" mock plum	185
" suet, plain	183
" " fruit	183
" " ginger	183

	PAGE		PAGE
Pudding, sponge	182	Blanc mange	190
" snow	186	" " farina	264
" Swedish	184	" " arrowroot	262
" Yorkshire	91	" " tapioca	263
Custards	175	" " banana	246
" apple	177	Sponge, strawberry	230
" baked	176	" raspberry	230
" cream meringue	232	Lemon snow	231
" chocolate	177	Chestnuts and cream	232
" "	176	Whipped cream	234
" fruit	176	Caramel	191
" orange	176		
" rice	179	PUDDING SAUCES.	
" tapioca	178	Sauces for puddings	192
" timbales	178	" caramel	193
" soft or boiled	175	" custard	194
" sponge cake in	245	" chocolate	193
Snow balls	185	" creamy	192
" " apple	184	" foamy	192
Fried cake	246	" fruit	193
Cake fritters	246	" hard	192
Apple scalloped	180	" " with fruit	194
" meringue	180	" lemon	192
" scalloped	180	" orange	193
" compote	180	Lemon syrup for waffles	193
" snow	191		
" atalanta	219	CAKE.	
Floating island	175	Cake	195
Orange Charlotte	186	" baking	195
		" currant	198
JELLIES, CREAMS, AND BLANC MANGE.		" cup	199
		" cocoanut layer	200
		" chocolate	200
Jelly, apples in	191	" raisin "	200
" lemon	190	" " " No. 2	200
" orange	191	" nut "	199
Bavarian cream	188	" " layer	199
" " chocolate	189	" orange layer	200
" " orange	189	" " filling	200
" " strawberry	190	" cream "	201
Mousse, chocolate	188	" lady	202
" fruit	187	" layer	199
Apple and meringue	245	" lunch	198
" " cream	245	" " currant and raisin	198
" snow	191	" " currant	198
Raspberry trifle	204	" fried	246
Jellied "	204	" fritters	246
Chantilly basket	204	" sponge	202
Orange charlotte	186	" " No. 2	202
" filled with jelly	187	" strawberry shortcake	203
" baskets	187	" raspberry "	203

INDEX.

	PAGE		PAGE
Cake, peach shortcake	202	Sherbet	215
" molasses fruit	201	" orange	215
Gingerbread	196	" lemon	216
" soft molasses	197	" " ginger	216
Ginger snaps	197	" strawberry	216
Soft molasses cookies	196	" raspberry	216
Doughnuts	196	" grape	217
" New England	197	Pineapple Ice	216
Boiled Icing	203	Cafe parfait	217
Ornamental Frosting	203		
Chantilly Basket	203		

FRUIT.

PASTRY AND PIES.

	PAGE		PAGE
		Apple and cream	245
		" " meringue	245
Pastry	205	" scalloped	180
Pie Apple	206	" snow	191
" cherry	207	" compote	180
" huckleberry	207	" baked	218
" lemon meringue	207	" sauce	218
" " " filling for	207	" Atalanta	219
" pumpkin	207	" for luncheon	219
" plain mince	208	Raspberry trifle	204
Puff paste	205	Compote of pears	245
Tarts	208	Stewed prunes	220
" cranberry	209	" cranberries	220
" lemon meringue	208	" fruit	220
" peach à la Italian	209	Fruit	218
Patties	208	" baskets	221
" Dresden cases	227	" to serve	218
Dumplings, Apple	209	"	218
		" meringue	220

ICE CREAMS AND SHERBETS.

	PAGE		PAGE
		Raspberry snow	222
		Berry cases	221
Freezing	210	Stuffed apples	232
Cream to mold	211	" pears	233
Ice cream and sherbet	210	Ambrosia	232
" vanilla	212	Orange compote	234
" chocolate	212	To prepare an orange	265
" coffee	212	Grated pineapple	222
" banana	212		
" lemon	212		
" apricot	213	### BEVERAGES.	
" bisque	213	Beverages	223
" strawberry	213	Coffee	223
" Philadelphia	214	" boiled	223
" peach	213	" filtered	223
" caramel	214	" cafe noir	224
" Delmonico	214	Tea	224
" tutti frutti	215	Chocolate	224
Frozen apricots	217	Cocoa	224
" fruits, see apricots	217	Lemonade	225
" custard	215	Orangeade	225

SUNDRIES.

	PAGE
Sundries	226
Bread crumbs	226
" " buttered	226
" sautéd	227
Cracker crumbs	226
" toasted	227
" and cheese	227
Croutons	227
Dresden patty cases	227
Toasted bread cases	228
Ham toast	228
Clam chowder	73
Fried smelts	79
Boiled fish	78
Drippings	228
Braised beef	228
Pot roast "	229
Panned chicken	229
Stewed celery	230
Raisin and rice pudding	230
Lemon snow	231
Caramel	191
Strawberry sponge	231
Raspberry "	231
Sweet omelet	231
Custard cream meringue	232
Chestnuts and cream	232
Stuffed apples	233
" pears	233
Ambrosia	233
Salted almonds	234
" peanuts	234
Orange compote	234
Whipped cream	234
Jellied trifle	235
Welsh rarebit	235
Company	264
To prepare canned vegetables	266
To stone raisins	266
To clean currants	266
" prepare lettuce	267
" " cucumbers	267
" " celery	267
Questions on lessons	268

ODDS AND ENDS.

	PAGE
Odds and ends	236
Picked-up soup	236
Warmed-up salmon	236
Plain hash	236
Vegetable hash	237
Corned beef balls	237
Pressed meat	237
Corned beef hash	237
" " " No. 2	238
" " " No. 3	238
Scalloped veal	238
Sliced beef with tomato sauce	239
Picked-up chicken	239
Cold chops with tomato sauce	239
Scalloped ham and chicken	239
" turkey	240
Warmed-up sweet potatoes	240
Rice balls	240
" and cheese	241
" fritters	241
Hominy pudding	241
" breakfast cakes	241
Oatmeal " "	241
Rice " "	241
Tomato and rice	243
Italian eggs	242
Cornstarch pudding	242
Bread and currant pudding	243
Apple and rice "	244
" " bread and butter pudding	244
" " meringue	245
" " cream	245
Compote of pears	245
Sponge cake in custard	245
Fried cake	246
Cake fritters	246
Banana blanc mange	246

INVALID COOKING.

	PAGE
Invalid cooking	247
How to care for the sick	248
Oatmeal gruel	249
" No. 2	250
Farina "	250
Barley "	250
Arrowroot "	250
Cracker "	251
Oatmeal mush	251
Hominy "	251
Panada	251
" No. 2	251
Oatmeal porridge	252
Milk "	252

	PAGE		PAGE
Oyster tea	252	Beef Tea bottled	257
" " No. 2	252	" juice	257
Pan broiled oysters	252	" broth	257
Creamed "	253	Mutton "	258
Roasted "	253	Chicken broth	258
Clam broth	253	" custard	259
" sauce on toast	254	Beef tea "	259
Boiled rice with milk	254	Farina	258
Rice-flour milk	254	Tapioca cream	259
Biscuits and "	254	Orange "	260
Softened biscuits	254	Cream cornstarch pudding	260
Toast	255	Arrowroot blanc-mange	260
" water	255	Tapioca " "	261
" milk	255	Rice custard	261
" " No. 2	255	Farina blanc-mange	262
" custard	255	Jellied rice	262
Raw beef sandwiches	256	Currant ice	263
Toasted crackers	256	Frozen beef tea	263
Crackers and marmalade	256	Jelly and ice	263
Beef tea	257	To prepare an orange	263

ADDITIONAL RECIPES.

PET OF THE HOUSEHOLD.

★ THE GREAT MEDICINAL FOOD ★

IMPERIAL GRANUM

PURE, DELICIOUS, NOURISHING

FOOD

FOR NURSING MOTHERS, INFANTS AND

CHILDREN

FOR **INVALIDS** AND CONVALESCENTS,
FOR DYSPEPTIC, DELICATE, INFIRM AND
AGED PERSONS
AN UNRIVALLED FOOD IN THE
SICK-ROOM

SOLD BY DRUGGISTS.  SHIPPING DEPOT— JOHN CARLE & SONS, NEW YORK.

The writer has a child that is as strong an argument for the use of IMPERIAL GRANUM as any mother could wish, and we therefore speak from experience when we say that it is both safe and nutritious, and it is the testimony of thousands of mothers who have brought up their children on IMPERIAL GRANUM that this preparation is successful where many others fail.—*The Christian Union.*

Sold by Druggists. Shipping Depot, JOHN CARLE & SONS, New York.

PILLSBURY'S FLOUR
MAKES
More Bread,
Better Bread,
Whiter Bread,
THAN ANY OTHER FLOUR.

Daily Product of the Pillsbury Mills,

17,500 BARRELS.

SOLD ✦ BY ✦ ALL ✦ GROCERS.

Don't Scold the Cook if Dinner is Spoiled.

IT MAY BE YOU ARE USING A POORLY CONSTRUCTED RANGE.

Look into the Merits of the

PERFECT RANGE.

Always on time and pleases the cooks.

Fitted with the celebrated Wrought Iron Adjustable Ventilated French Pastry and roasting ovens. Ten years in advance of any range in the market. Correspondence solicited.

RICHARDSON & BOYNTON CO.,
232 and 234 Water St., New York.

WALTER BAKER & CO.'S
BREAKFAST COCOA

PROFESSOR JAMES F. BABCOCK, the well-known chemical expert, for many years State Assayer for Massachusetts, recently purchased in open market a sample of WALTER BAKER & CO.'S BREAKFAST COCOA, and, after making a careful analysis, filed the following certificate :—

BOSTON, JANUARY 20, 1892.

THIS certifies that I have made a very thorough chemical and microsopic examination of the article known as WALTER BAKER & CO.'S BREAKFAST COCOA, and I have compared the results with those found from a similar examination of the pure roasted cocoa-bean.

I find that WALTER BAKER & CO.'S BREAKFAST COCOA is *absolutely pure*. It contains no trace of any substance foreign to the pure roasted cocoa-bean. The color is that of pure cocoa. The flavor is natural, and not artificial ; and the product is in every particular such as must have been produced from the pure cocoa-bean without the addition of any chemical, alkali, acid, or artificial flavoring substance which are to be detected in cocoas prepared by the so-called "Dutch process."

[Signed]   JAMES F. BABCOCK.

Ask your Grocer for it. Allow no Substitution.

WALTER BAKER & CO.,   -   **DORCHESTER, MASS.**

Indispensable to good housekeeping.—*Emma P. Ewing.*

(Size 14½ inches long by 1½ inches wide.)

This knife is in a class by itself.
Nothing approaches it in point of efficacy, durability and simplicity.
It is indispensable to good housekeeping.
From tip to tip it is solid steel of finest quality, beautifully finished and plated.
It is not a machine, but a knife.
Sharpened exactly like any other knife on a whetstone or steel.
Cuts thick or thin slices, hot or cold.
Shall we send you one at our expense of express or mail, for seventy-five cents?
You can return it the same way and get your money if you don't want it.

THERE ARE IMITATIONS.

CHRISTY KNIFE CO.,
Fremont, Ohio.

CALL AND SEE

OUR NEW STORE,

Flatbush Ave., Fulton and Nevins Streets,

BROOKLYN.

The Largest Furniture and Carpet House in the City.

Stocked with a full and complete assortment of Everything for Housekeeping.

LOW PRICES.   RELIABLE GOODS.

ONLY 10 PER CENT. CASH DOWN.

50c. weekly or $2.00 monthly on $30.00.
75c. weekly or $3.00 monthly on $50.00.
$1.00 weekly or $4.00 monthly on $65.00.
$1.25 weekly or $5.00 monthly on $80.00.
$1.50 weekly or $6.00 monthly on $100.00.
Larger amounts on terms to suit purchaser's convenience.

COWPERTHWAIT CO.,

Flatbush Ave., Fulton and Nevins Sts.,

BROOKLYN.

www.ingramcontent.com/pod-product-compliance
Lightning Source LLC
Chambersburg PA
CBHW022028240426
43667CB00042B/1242